LIFE LOOKS UP

LIFE LOOKS UP

by

CHARLES B. TEMPLETON

HARPER & BROTHERS PUBLISHERS

NEW YORK

Library of Congress catalog card number: 54-12812

TO CONNIE

CONTENTS

INTRODUCTION   9

1. THE FAMILIAR STRANGER   13

2. REVOLUTION!—CHRISTIAN STYLE   27

3. THE BIGGER THEY COME   41

4. HOW TO BE GOOD THE EASY WAY   53

5. LAND OF BEGINNING AGAIN   67

6. LIFE LOOKS UP   79

7. LIFE CAN BE BEAUTIFUL—IF   93

8. CHROME-PLATED CHAOS   105

9. MAKING YOUR LIFE COUNT   119

10. TRADING PEARLS FOR PEBBLES   133

11. SAINT WITH MUSCLES   147

12. GOD BELIEVES IN YOU   159

13. MAKING RELIGION REAL   171

14. THE END IS THE BEGINNING   183

INTRODUCTION

WHAT a task—to preach to Americans. A minister would need
to be either a consummate egotist or a man of faith. Philip
Bailey has called the United States

> . . . half-brother of the world,
> With something good and bad of every land.

What an intimidating task—to try to bring the Christian gospel to contemporary America. What a task even to understand
America—complex, contradictory colossus that she is; seething, yeasting, vital organism that she is. Who can claim fully
to understand a nation which within one hundred years has
grown from a primitive country to the wealthiest and mightiest
power in history?

Who can begin to understand a nation so full of paradox?
A nation that can produce an Abraham Lincoln and a Hughie
Long, a Franklin Roosevelt and a Frankie Sinatra, a George
Washington Carver and a Father Divine, a John Singer Sar-
geant and an Al Capp, a Thomas Alva Edison and the inven-
tor of the Knee-Action Potato-Peeler? Who can pretend fully
to understand a nation that has the highest standard of living
in history and loves hot dogs, that has the finest symphony
orchestras and invents be-bop, that has the National Association for the Advancement of Colored People and the Ku-Klux

Klan, that builds a multi-billion dollar television industry and then uses it to broadcast soap opera?

Such is the tempo of American life that one is astonished Americans find the time to listen or to read at all. George Santayana has said, "All his life he [the American] jumps into the train after it has started and jumps out before it has stopped; and he never once gets left behind or breaks his leg." It is precisely this frenetic way of life that encourages one to believe these talks will be read. The national malaise of soul back of the current revival of interest in religion has been induced, in part, by the pressure and uncertainty of life in these United States in this atomic age.

One is further encouraged to hope these talks will prove helpful because some of them have already been given across the country to hundreds of thousands of people. Essentially, they are sermons, prepared to be preached to a cross section of society in language that is deliberately simple and nontheological. While it is hoped one has not sinned too grievously against the homiletician's art, these are actually not so much sermons as religious talks. They are sent out with the prayer that those who read them may be helped to understand and to follow after God.

Where quotations from the scriptures are used they are either from the King James or the Revised Standard Version.

Appreciation should be expressed to Mrs. Mildred Y. Losee, Mrs. Martha C. Door and Mrs. Lydia Minassian for their assistance in typing the manuscript.

CHARLES B. TEMPLETON

New York City, N. Y.

LIFE LOOKS UP

Don't be fooled by those hyperreligionists who go about as studiously sad as an undertaker, as doleful as a bloodhound and, usually, as negative and critical as can be. They are a denial of the very faith they profess. The worst enemies of the Church have always been those ultrapious people who act as though the proof of piety is sobriety and as though your goodness is in direct proportion to the number of your inhibitions.

❧ 1 ❧

THE FAMILIAR STRANGER

IF YOU were to meet Jesus walking down the street do you think you would recognize him? The chances are you would not. Despite the fact he is better known than anyone in history we have so lost contact with him across the centuries that, in all likelihood, he would seem as a stranger to most of us.

Not long ago I chanced across a book filled with reproductions of paintings and statues of Jesus. Most of the great works of art of which he was the subject were reproduced there. I turned the pages and saw representations by the hundreds. None was the same. In some he appeared gaunt and tall. Some pictured him as a beardless youth, others as a bent and aged patriarch. He frowned. He looked heavenward. He was reproachful. He was tender. In some he looked bland and effeminate; his robes in immaculate folds, a halo round his head and a hand uplifted in benediction. In others he was a glowering tyrant. In some of the modern painting he was unrecognizable. It seemed that few of the artists had caught anything of the dynamic passion that dwelt within him. Indeed, it seemed the artists had not so much revealed the Christ as themselves.

Even as the artists misrepresented him so do we. We all

have a mental picture of Jesus hanging in the art gallery of our imagination. There can be little doubt but what, in most cases, it is an inadequate one. Somehow, across the intervening years we have lost him. We have so sentimentalized and misunderstood him that it is likely he would never be recognized were he to walk our streets and speak to our problems.

Perhaps you doubt that. I did too until I went out onto the streets of a major American city and conducted an informal poll. I stopped people at random and put to them simple, basic questions about Jesus, his life and his teaching. It is understatement to say that I was astonished at the misinformation in the minds of the majority of those questioned. There are a number of reasons for our confusion concerning Christ. The first is arrested development. Many mature physically and intellectually while their religious concepts remain juvenile. They still think of God in Sunday School terms. Another reason is the misinterpretation of the American doctrine of the separation of Church and State. Too often it has been interpreted to mean the separation of *Religion* and the State, and we have the incredible spectacle of a nation founded on religious principles forbidding the explaining of these principles in her schools.

Many of our misconceptions grow out of unfamiliarity with the facts. Many who reject the Bible have never read it. Many sincere and intelligent people who contend they cannot accept the medieval ideas of the Church do not know what it is they are called upon to accept. Many vital young people who say Christianity is doleful and antiquated have no real understanding of what the Christian message comprises. In many instances the responsibility for these misconceptions lies at the door of the Church which has frequently mirrored a distorted faith.

Let us look at three of the most famous misconceptions about the Christian faith. First: that the Christian life is a sad and somber way of life.

C. S. Lewis, the Oxford don and author of so many helpful Christian books, tells of a schoolboy who was asked what he thought God was like. The boy answered that as far as he could make out, "God is the kind of person who is always snooping around to see if anyone is enjoying himself so he can put a stop to it." A lot of people have that idea of God. He is a cosmic killjoy, most pleased when His followers are properly lugubrious. Well, there *are* Christians who give that impression!

But Christ did not come to darken our lives and to steal from them all that is enticing and interesting and fun. Indeed, the message that heralded his birth was, "Behold I bring you good tidings of great joy. . . !" Too long has the Christian message been identified with gloom. The music that burst through the heavens was not a dirge but an anthem. It was the birth of a Baby not the funeral of good times. Let us have done with this idea that religion is dolorous and that when it enters the front door fun and laughter go out the back. Don't be fooled by those hyperreligionists who go about as studiously sad as an undertaker, as doleful as a bloodhound and, usually, as negative and critical as can be. They are a denial of the very faith they profess. The worst enemies of the Church have always been those ultrapious people who act as though the proof of piety is sobriety and as though your goodness is in direct proportion to the number of your inhibitions.

No amount of minuses can add up to that kind of "plus living" that Jesus demands. He did not come ". . . to condemn the world, but that the world, through him, might be saved." Jesus said, "I am come that ye might have life, and that more abundantly." He took the ten negative commandments of the Decalogue, added them up and got a total of two *positive* commands; "Thou shalt love the Lord thy God with all thy heart and thy neighbor as thyself." This then is the basis of a full-orbed Christian life: a love for God that puts worship at the heart of life and imparts a love for others and the desire to serve them. Being a Christian is not just a matter of getting your own little soul all fixed up and sitting around looking pious.

Can you not see this fundamental joyousness hinted at in the creation and, especially, in the flowers with which God has bedecked the continents? The brilliant colors of the flowers seem to shout in an exultant voice, "God is good and happiness is the sign of His presence. He loves bright and lovely things. He is not to be served in sadness and in fear but in an abandonment of radiant living. He is the God of color; of the rainbow, of the flowers, of the peacock and of the sunset." The abundance of the flowers seems to hint at the measure in which God gives His blessings. It is never in a meager way. When He gives water He pours it out in oceans and sparkling lakes and tumbling rivers. When He gives food he gives wheat in the fields, berries on the bush, fruit on the trees, honey in the comb. When he gives flowers—of no practical use save to beautify and make glad—he gives them by the billion, flaming in every forest, lining every stream, crowning every tree, snuggled in the grass . . . handfuls, armfuls, basketfuls and ten million to spare.

Despite this evidence to the contrary there are thousands who believe that to be Christian is to say good-by to all good times and to spend the rest of your life singing long-meter hymns in a cavernous cathedral or a drab mission hall. As George MacLeod suggests, "The man of humor thinks if he becomes a Christian he will have to cultivate solemnity. The man of ambition that he will have to forget his dreams. Many a man of business thinks he will have to resign his occupation and buy a tambourine. Many a youth thinks of Christianity as a long list of negatives to be countersigned and gloomily lived by. But the man of humor will have it reborn, not stifled. The man of ambition will let his vision loose in the Kingdom of God. The man of business will attend more, not less, to his business and will square it up with what he knows to be right, and the young person will finally find a cause to which he can devote the last ounce of his enthusiasm and loyalty."

But lest the wrong impression be left let it be clear that Christian joy is not an inane and irresponsible banishment of the seamy side of life. The true Christian is a realist. He is not surprised to come upon evil and ugliness; his world view tells him to expect it. He knows full well that

Life is real! Life is earnest!

He has no ivory tower into which he escapes when the going gets rough. But the Christian lives in a context of two worlds: the one he knows through his senses and the one he senses in his spirit. He is borne up in trouble by the promise that "in everything God works for good with them that love Him." And even if the world comes tumbling down about us—as it may well do in this atomic age—he remembers, "The Lord God omnipotent reigneth!" and holds the future in His hands! Rid your mind once and for all of the notion that Christianity is a sad and somber way of life. It is, as Jesus said it would be, "abundant" living.

Now to the second objection: that Christianity is a drab and unchallenging way of life.

Many a young person when challenged by the Church has responded, "Become a Christian? I should say not. What red-blooded young person wants to spend his life carrying around a big black Bible and sitting in a sparse audience— mostly women and elderly people—discussing ancient tales about the Hittites and the Amorites and the . . . what-chamacallites, or tracing the ancestry of some ancient and unlamented King through a half a hundred 'begats'? This is a great time to be alive, when there are so many things to be done and so many interesting things to be a part of. The last thing I want to do is to sit around in some gloomy church and talk about love and joy and peace. I want to live! I want a challenge for my life; something that will grip me in a great compulsion. Christianity is too tame, too dull."

To this I would respond, "I don't blame you. You are dead right. If Christianity is what you have pictured it to be I would not want any part of it either. The trouble is we are discussing two different things. You are thinking of a counterfeit that is too often passed off in the name of Christianity—but is a long, sea mile removed from the real thing—and I am talking about the kind of life that Jesus Christ revealed when he was here on earth."

At its best there is nothing in all the world that can stand in the same company with the Church. But too often it has not been at its best. Too often the Church has given the impression that it is designed to preserve the status quo, that its principal mission is to create patience and resignation, to bury the dead, to talk in an unnatural way about the world to come and to have too little that is relevant to say about the world we live in. Too often the Church has lost its stringent note and has seemed eager to appease the State and the world. Sometimes it has even let evils flourish in its shadow. And the man on the street has looked on and has seen no reason to be challenged.

But there are many churches that are not like this. Those who stand on the outside just do not know. The early Church certainly was not like this! Back there it was the center of attraction for the courageous and to belong to it was to take your life in your hands. Society was secure and Christianity was dangerous. Beyond doubt those early Christians had something—and there are thousands who have it today, make no mistake about that. They had something that was changing the world. They had a cause that was supreme. They followed behind the most heroic Leader in history. They marched under the noblest banner of all time. And it is to this the Church calls us today!

No challenge in Christianity? A young Englishman, in the early days of the war, was a conscientious objector. He finally changed his mind and joined the Royal Air Force. He gave as his reason the fact that he could not bear watching the bombs smashing English houses, breaking up English homes and destroying English lives. Well, there is another war on, and too many are standing apart from it. Perhaps if we could see the way it is destroying American homes in the divorce court, wrecking young lives in the slums and debauching America's youth in a hundred ways, *we* would not be able to stand aside either.

Even more surely than bombs destroy, sin destroys! Is that mere ministerial mumbo jumbo? No, it is stark, grim reality; as a trip through the V. D. ward of any hospital or through the deep slums of any city will convince you. There is a war on . . . a bitter, desperate, long-lived, relentless war! A war between right and wrong, between good and evil, between God and anti-God. Where do you stand?

Talk about a challenge! Where is there a challenge like it? To stand for the right, to align oneself with Almighty God, to march under the command of Christ, to be a part of the solution rather than a part of the problem, to bring peace, encouragement and strength, and the glad good news that God has come to redeem and to make life over again.

Finally, we come to the third objection: that Christianity is a restricted and negative way of life.

We live at a time when the emphasis is on freedom. The man of today does not want any restrictions on his life. "I shall not become a Christian," he says, "because it is a negative life. It is a series of prohibitions, a life full of thou shalt nots, and I just won't have my life shackled and inhibited by a thousand ancient restraints."

Let this be crystal clear: the essence of the Christian gospel is anything but negative. You may have heard it proclaimed otherwise but, in the words of Gershwin's little song, "It ain't necessarily so!" No amount of negations will make you Christian. All the minuses in the world can never add up to the kind of plus living that Jesus demands. You can take out of your life a half a hundred things that people tell you are wrong and it will not make you Christian—it will merely make you empty.

Jesus did not come to restrict and to bind, but to free—and "whom the Son sets free is free indeed." He added up the "thou shalt nots" of the Decalogue and the total was positive, not negative: "Thou shalt love the Lord thy God with all thy heart and thy neighbor as thyself." *That* is the gospel! Not restricted living, not negative prohibitions, but warm, positive living.

There is altogether too much careless talk about freedom.

There has been a strong emphasis on self-expression (Archbishop William Temple felt that any artist who insisted on expressing his self ought to see to it that he had a self worth expressing), and in seeing one necessary side of the picture we have failed to remember the other. Self-expression may be necessary for the full-flowered life but so is discipline. One recalls how in art school it was pointed out that a painting is great not only because of what it includes but also because of what it leaves out.

Life demands certain restrictions. We cannot say "yes" to certain things in life unless we are ready to say "no" to other things. Those who want to say "yes" to a sylphlike figure know they can do so only by saying "no" to starchy desserts and sweets. Young people must say "no" to lazy, adventurous evenings or they cannot say "yes" to passing grades in their examinations. Young ladies cannot say "yes" to that new spring outfit unless they say "no" to a number of little purchases they would like to make. Life demands certain restrictions and there is no freedom except in conformity to law. As Harry Emerson Fosdick has pointed out, take away the stop-light system from the main intersection of the city and you do not get freedom you get chaos.

It is a fact that none of us is free. We say, "This is a free country therefore I can do as I please." The statement is correct but the conclusion is not. This *is* a free country but you cannot do as you please. If anyone thinks that because he is free he is free to do as he pleases, let him speed down the main street of any city at seventy miles per hour and see how long he remains free. Feel free to help yourself from the cash drawer at the bank and you will soon find that your freedom is limited. The simple fact is that we are not free to do as we please; we are only free within the laws of our being or our society. A fish is not free to live on the land. A bird is not free to live under water. Without special equipment a man is not free to live on the surface of the moon. We are free within certain restrictions, but the restrictions are for our good.

There are some who argue that the Christian faith circumscribes a life. Certainly there are restrictions in the Christian life but they are the restrictions of love. They are designed for our advantage not to narrow life's borders. Two boys of the same age live in the same city. One lives in the residential section in a home characterized by parental love and care. The other boy lives "on the other side of the tracks" in a broken home. His mother is a slatternly woman with no concern except for her own convenience. As night falls the first boy is sent off to bed. He chafes under the restriction and grumbles as he goes. The other boy is free to run the streets as he wishes. Which of the two boys is "free" to grow up to a good and useful adulthood—the boy who is restricted by the love of his parents or the waif who slips down the grimy back stairs of the tenement where he lives to roam the dark streets and alleys through the night?

Jesus said, "Take my yoke upon you." That sounds confining and we draw back. But he goes on to say, "For my yoke is easy and my burden is light." There are restrictions in the

Christian life but it is a happy bondage. It is something akin to marriage. The marriage ceremony speaks of "the *bonds* of holy matrimony," and the word is appropriate. A married man is not free. But go to a happily married man and offer him his freedom. He is not interested. He doesn't want to date other women. He is perfectly happy to be restricted to one woman and one home. Indeed, he realizes that it is in this restriction that he is able to bring his life to fulfillment. It is a happy bondage, as is the Christian life.

Then let us bring this radiant faith out of the shadows. Let us become acquainted anew with Jesus, and this time let us see him as he really is. Perhaps, if we can shake off some of our misconceptions, we too will run with something of the breathless excitement of Andrew to cry, "We have found him! We have found him. . . !"

If we in the Western world are to meet the challenge with which we are confronted we will have to rediscover the spiritual basis of our political ideas. It will be "this nation under God" or this nation under the heel of a dictator, foreign born or domestic. This is a day of revolution. The world is in ferment, full of seething, yeasting forces, and we must make the revolution of our time a Christian revolution.

❧ 2 ❧

REVOLUTION!—CHRISTIAN STYLE

THE history of the world has been altered by the events which took place in two small rooms, separated by thousands of miles and thousands of years. This is the story of those two "upper rooms" and the influences that have flowed from them.

The first of these rooms is in London, England. In the Soho district, one of the slum sections of that great city, the hour is late and everyone is abed. From the second-story window of a drab flat over a dingy laundry, light seeps into the foggy street. Through a dirty and curtainless window you peer into the room. In the center of the room stands a round table. Piled on top of the table is a strange conglomeration of odds and ends: a pile of tattered manuscripts, a pipe amid some scattered ashes, a teacup with a broken handle, a child's toy, some odds and ends from a woman's work basket.

Seated at the table, writing with a fierce intensity, is a man. The guttering lamp above his head seems to etch even deeper the dark, harsh lines in his face. He has fierce jutting eyebrows and a black bushy beard. He writes on through the night, the only sound in the room the scratching of the cheap pen in his hand.

27

His name is Karl Marx. He is the father of modern communism and he is writing *Das Kapital,* the bible of modern communism. Out of this upper room in London flowed influences that have changed the history of the world; a doctrine of strife and duplicity that has already taken the lives of millions of men and women . . . and the end is not yet!

The other upper room is in one of the oldest cities in the world, Jerusalem. Crowded together in it are one hundred and twenty men and women, the disciples of Jesus of Nazareth, gathered there in obedience to one of his last commands. They are very ordinary people; average, unexciting, illiterate people. Suddenly, into their expectant hearts—in a mystery that none can explain or explain away—there comes the Spirit of Christ and they are transformed.

Out of that upper room in Jerusalem flowed influences that have changed the history of the world—a gospel of love and brotherhood that has already taken the lives of millions of men and women and transformed them . . . and again, the end is not yet!

Our world stands today in doubt and indecision looking at these two upper rooms and at the influences that have flowed from them across the years. The world is sick, seriously, critically sick, and all kinds of radical remedies have been proposed. It is said that we need a revolution. Indeed we do! —but not as the Communists are propounding it. We need, instead, a revolution . . . *Christian style!*

Perhaps someone remonstrates to say, "These are strange

words from a follower of Jesus. What in the world has Jesus— of all people, Jesus—to do with such warlike terms as 'revolution'? Surely you can't be serious, the gentle Jesus is no revolutionary! Isn't he the 'meek and lowly Nazarene,' the 'lover of our souls,' the 'fairest of ten thousand'? What in the world has the gentle Christ to do with such things as revolution?"

To think of him in these terms is to reveal that we have lost sight of him with the passage of the centuries. Jesus is the most dynamic and revolutionary figure the world has ever seen. It is true that when Jesus was born the heavens were filled with the song, "Peace on earth . . ." but never forget the Babe grew to manhood to cry, "I have come not to bring peace . . . but a sword; to be a divider among men . . . to kindle a fire upon the earth!" We forget that when Jesus stood on trial the only charge they could lay against him in which there was any element of truth was the charge, "He stirreth up the people!" They were right. He did. He always has when men have understood him and heeded him. He is a disturber. He took the cross and, using it as a pry and Calvary as a fulcrum, turned the world upside down! And his disciples followed in his train. This was the charge against them, "These men that have turned the world upside down have come here also!"

Let it be said, first, that we need a revolution in the Church. This is not to join the chorus of the critics of the Church. It would seem that any hope for a peaceful, purposeful future is ultimately dependent upon the Church. But, having avowed one's faith in and loyalty to the Church, it must be said that we need a revolution in the Church; a revolution from the grass-roots to the highest echelons, from the humblest member to the most dignified ecclesiastic, a revolution that will rouse us from our torpor and call us to the heroic dedication of mind and heart our age demands.

That there are splendid individual churches and a general stirring of revival everywhere is evident, but how impotent and inept we so often are. In attendance: more than 86 million members on the rolls but only 30 million of America's 160 million population regularly at worship. Our Bible: how proud we are that year after year it is far and away the "best seller" (even in the Germany of 1939 it outsold Hitler's *Mein Kampf*) but how pitifully little it is read and how tragically little it is understood. In moral power: the growth of the Church is faster than the growth of the population but the added numerical strength is not evident in an increase in moral power. The statistical columns reveal a nation increasingly Christian, the news columns reveal a mounting paganism.

This is particularly tragic because of the crisis of our time. We stand at the crossroads of the centuries. There can be little doubt but what historians will regard this as one of the most momentous periods in history. Every border between the behemoths of the Communist and the Western world bristles with bayonets. The race to arm goes on at an ever-accelerating pace even while the destructive potential mounts like a mushrooming cloud. At the heart of the growing tension, twentieth-century man lives out his uncertain days with growing apprehensiveness and profound uncertainty.

Our dilemma is, in part, the result of the failure of the Church. Our refusal to love, to share our faith and our wealth with the pagan and the poor of the world has left a vacuum into which the Communists have moved. The great scandal of our generation is the fact that the Communists are strongest in nations where once the Church was established and where up to 99 per cent of the citizens of the country were baptized members of the Church.

Christians have been guilty of a kind of isolationism. We have been like the priests in the New Testament story to whom Judas came after the betrayal. His face twisted in remorse and self-revulsion, he hurled the thirty pieces of silver to the floor and they skimmed and rolled in a dozen directions. Then, turning to the priests, he cried out, "I have sinned in that I have betrayed innocent blood!" And what was the response of these men who had bribed him to do the deed? They coldly turned their backs and walked away. "What is that to us?" they said. "See thou to that!" That's your business, not ours!

And have we not done the same? When Hitler and Mussolini began to tell the world their dreams we said, "What is that to us?"—and soon their dreams became our nightmare. When some of the underfed nations of the world began to cry out for a more equal ration we said, "What is that to us?" —and soon we were all being rationed. When the Japanese had a revival of Shintoism and attacked China we said, "What is that to us?"—and soon our own sons were dying with the

Chinese in the Pacific. When the Russians laughed God out of court, sneered at the Bible and appointed themselves champions of the underprivileged we said, "What is that to us?"—and now we are beginning to see it is a matter of life and death to us!

Jesus commanded us to love our neighbor and for a long time we thought this was a pleasant religious option. We are beginning to realize it is an absolute, imperative "must." Today it is "love thy neighbor" or else! In a world that has become a neighborhood but not a brotherhood nothing that happens anywhere can be dismissed by saying, "That's their funeral," for it is likely to be ours too!

We must come awake to the realization that the problems of the world are our problems and we must bring Christian compassion and Christian helpfulness to them. Christianity is not the mere salvation of the individual soul, it is the demonstration of God's love in human life. To find that love is to want to share it. God never fills a life but what He overflows it. It is one thing to cry, "What must I do to be saved?" but we must go on to cry, "What must I do to save?" Gripped in a great compulsion we must shake off our lethargy and move out to serve the needs of men.

There is a great reluctance among Christians to dedicate themselves to service. There is nothing romantic in some of the disagreeable tasks that demand doing and because they require "blood and sweat and tears" we are loath to begin. There is no point in deluding ourselves, the service of God

and man costs. It means sacrifice. It is often unpleasant, unnoticed and unappreciated, and because it is we draw back.

There is nothing strange in this reluctance. It is abnormal
to want to sacrifice. The psychiatrist will know what is wrong
with the person who *wants* to sacrifice. It needs to be clearly
understood that Jesus did not *want* to die. No one wants to die
unless he is already dead on the inside, and Jesus was more
fully alive than anyone has ever been. This was no masochistic
seeking of suffering. Jesus did not want to die. We forget that
he was young in years when he went to the cross. He was
but thirty-three and the tides of life surged strong within him.
That was the reason for the awful struggle in Gethsemane;
not a momentary struggle but a prolonged, soul-racking
struggle that, in its intensity, brought the sweat to his brow in
great globules "like as blood." Not the struggle of a moment
but one hours long and agonizing. He did not want to
sacrifice himself—of course not! Who but a madman would
seek the welter of blood and agony that was the cross? He did
not want to lay down his life . . . *but he did it!*

They asked a missionary about to return to Africa whether
he liked his work. He turned to the questioner and said quietly,
"Of course I don't like my work. We are people of average
sensitivity and we don't like dirt and infestation and danger
and isolation from our loved ones, but Heaven help our world
if we only do for God what we *like* to do!"

There must be a revolution in the Church. We must stop
"playing Church." It is not enough to be ordinary Christians
in these extraordinary times. Christianity is not a matter of

mere church membership, or sitting in a pew singing some pleasant little hymns, or remembering to say one's prayers. Christianity is a great compulsion that thrusts you to the heart of the world's problems and empowers you to do something to solve them. We must have men and women who take God seriously in a serious time and who will go out to turn the world upside down for God.

But if there is to be a revolution in the Church it can only happen when there is a revolution in the individual. In the words of Robert Frost, the call is

> . . . to a one man revolution,
> The only revolution that is coming

Our calamity lies in the fact that the Communits are beating us at the very thing in which we specialize. The Church has always specialized in consecration, yet the Communists are outconsecrating us. That is, in part, the explanation for their incredible growth. In one generation they have won 37 per cent of the world's population. Eight hundred million people are under their sway. The Communist is a great "believer." He is convinced that his cause is right, that he cannot fail, and he is ready to live or die for his beliefs.

As Arnold Toynbee has pointed out, it is impossible to understand the conflict in our world unless we understand that the basic issues are religious. It is not so much a conflict of armed might as it is a battle of ideologies, a contest between two great faiths. Communism can never be understood until it is seen for what it is: a great, nonsupernaturalistic world

faith. Communism is avowedly and officially atheistic, but though it may have thrown away the trappings of traditional religion it has erected in their place a faith that has all the elements of a religion.

For instance, they have the Communist equivalent of God: their God is "dialectical materialism," which they believe is a logical, impersonal, ongoing force at the heart of the cosmos, a law with which they are in tune and thus they believe they cannot fail. They have the Communist equivalent of the Scriptures: their holy books are the writing of Marx, Engels and Stalin. They take orthodoxy very seriously. If you are guilty of heresy—deviationism—they do not excommunicate you, they "liquidate" you, which is much more permanent. They have the equivalent of disciples: men and women who live disciplined and dedicated lives and who are ready, as millions have demonstrated, to lay down their lives for their beliefs. They have the equivalent of a messiah: Nikolay Lenin, who, subsequent to his "wilderness experience" in Switzerland, traveled across Germany in a sealed and armored train to spark the revolution in Russia. They have the equivalent of a holy sepulcher: in the Red Square in Moscow the bodies of Lenin and Stalin lie embalmed, and to this place millions of Russians make pilgrimage every year. They have the equivalent of missionaries: men and women who have gone into all the world to spread their beliefs and who, in one generation, have reached every nation and have infiltrated every level of society.

The Western world, faced with this enormous challenge, has frequently fallen subject to the illusion that communism can be defeated by military might. But if history has demonstrated any one thing beyond contradiction it has demonstrated this: you can't stop an idea with guns and tanks and bombs. You can't destroy an idea by shooting the man who holds it. Nor can you halt it by putting those who believe in it in jail (never forget that Hitler wrote *Mein Kampf* while behind prison bars in Germany). Surely a nation with a Christian heritage should know this; was not Jesus crucified? Were not his disciples martyred, his followers imprisoned, exiled and persecuted?—and yet the Christian faith spread. Whether the idea be good or evil you cannot stop it with force.

There is only one way to defeat an idea and that is with a better idea, and the only idea in the world today with the vitality inherent within it needed to defeat communism is the democratic idea!

But democracy is a meaningless word apart from faith in God. As we have seen again and again, liberty, justice, freedom and human rights become meaningless words when faith in God goes from the heart of a nation. You get your concept of man from your concept of God. If you do not believe in God then human personality is not sacred, the end justifies the means, the State becomes supreme and all the evils of the totalitarians become possible. But if you believe in God, then human personality is sacred and one man's liberty, one man's freedom, one man's rights are more important than any institution, and democracy becomes more than a word to be twisted to the dictator's purpose.

It is not by chance that freedom dies in a nation that forgets

God; it is inevitable. You can see in contemporary Germany what happens when materialism is carried to its logical conclusion. At the turn of the century Germany led the world in culture, in the arts and in the sciences. Then the nation cast aside her faith in God and began to shout their hosannas to their "Father"—Der Führer. Suddenly liberty was gone, barbarism became dominant and decency died. Think back to the Jewish pogroms, to the unbelievable horror of Belsen and Buchenwald, to those indescribable pictures of emaciated men and women stacked like so much cordwood awaiting the fire! All this in a "civilized" nation!

The evils that are part and parcel of communism are the direct and inevitable result of their faith. The Communist believes that God is a superstition, that truth is relative, that morals are a matter of expediency, that life has no transcendent meaning and that the grave is the end. Is it strange then that freedom in the Soviet Union is limited, that cruelty is commonplace, that millions of peasants were deliberately allowed to starve during the twenties, that a reliable estimate puts the number of prisoners in the forced-labor camps at seventeen million and that deception and "the big lie" are common practice in diplomacy?

If there is no God to be accounted to and a man is not your neighbor but someone to step on on the way to what you want, then why not take life by the throat and take from it everything you can get, and let the devil take the hindmost? But when you believe in God, when you believe that life is a trust, that human personality is sacred, that morality is not

37

relative but finally and irrevocably fixed, and that the will of God will certainly and ultimately prevail, then liberty and justice and freedom mean something.

If we in the Western world are to meet the challenge with which we are confronted we will have to rediscover the spiritual basis of our political ideas. It will be "this nation under God" or this nation under the heel of a dictator, foreign born or domestic. This is a day of revolution. The world is in ferment, full of seething, yeasting forces, and we must make the revolution of our time a Christian revolution.

But the issue is personal. Nations are men and the strength and weakness of a nation reflect the strength and weakness of her people. America will not change until we are changed. The world will be no different until we are different. The Chinese have a proverb, "If you want a clean city, clean up your own front yard." It might be restated to say, "If you want a better world, clean up your own life!" We are a part of the problem or we are a part of the solution.

What can we do? What can any individual do in a world caught in the grip of great forces? Some years ago a great convocation of people, one hundred thousand in number, met in the Los Angeles Coliseum. Suddenly, in the midst of the program, every light went out. Before anyone could panic a voice boomed over the loud-speakers to say, "Don't be alarmed. We turned out the lights for a purpose. Do this; each one of you get a match. If you haven't one, borrow one, but each one get a match and hold it in your hand." Then when the noise had subsided the voice came again, "When I give the signal,

light your match and hold it up until it burns itself out."
Then, after a pause the voice rang out again, "Light your
match!"

At first there were just a few flickering fireflies of light in
that great bowl of blackness. Then the bowl became a glowing
jewel box of light. Suddenly it burst into a great blaze of light,
seeming by contrast brighter than the light of day. Then,
slowly, the light wavered, flickered, pinpointed out and died.
The crowd sat silent in the darkness, a darkness that seemed
the darker by contrast. Then, in the great silence, the voice
asked, "What did you do? You lit one match. One little,
flickering, short-lived match . . . nothing in this great sea
of darkness. But when all of us did the same it became a light
brighter than the noonday sun!" Then, in the words of Jesus,
the voice went on, "Even so, let your light shine before men,
that they may see your good works and glorify your Father
which is in Heaven!"

What can we do to meet the challenge of our day? This
at least we can do: we can let our light shine, feeble as it
may seem in the great darkness of our day! We can let men
see our lives, clear and radiant and pure, the reflection of the
Light of the World. And if we will, dozens and thousands
of others may join us until a light is kindled that will break
through the great darkness—the overarching darkness—of
our time. Then, "Let *your* light so shine before men, that they
may see *your good works,* and glorify your Father which is in
heaven!"

Are we meeting the unparalleled challenge of our time with dedication and imagination, or are we asleep? With too many it is "life as usual" in a world bursting at the seams. Ours is a day that demands greatness and heroic resolve, and yet we sleep!

❧ 3 ❧

THE BIGGER THEY COME

THERE is an ancient myth about the Greek hero Achilles relating how his mother—anxious to keep him from the wounds of battle—anointed him with ambrosia and dipped him in the river Styx, thus making him impervious to the wounds of battle. However, in order to dip the child she had to hold onto his heel and he was thus left vulnerable at this one spot. He was finally killed when an arrow struck him in his one place of weakness, his heel.

Even as with Achilles, the strong of every age have their weak points, the wise prove fallible and the mighty go down to defeat. There is a chink in everyone's armor. All have their weaknesses; the captains and the kings, the prophet and the disciple. To this fact the incontrovertible record of history bears witness.

This is the story of two men: Samson, whose life is recorded in the pages of the Old Testament, and Peter, a disciple of Jesus. Few men have reached such heights, few have duplicated their insights, few have demonstrated such a capacity for leadership, and few have failed so utterly, so resoundingly.

Regard these two men for a moment. What intriguing figures they are. Samson! Peter! How their very names set the imagination afire! Samson would be a standout in any day. Can you picture how it would be if he were alive today? Ours is a generation that greatly admires physical prowess and who can say that Samson would not outshine even such heroes as Rocky Marciano and Ted Williams and Bob Mathias? In your imagination see him as he once was. There he goes, walking with the imperious assurance of the man who knows he has no peer: unshorn hair, bulging biceps, bronzed and radiantly healthy, knowing the favor of both God and man. There he stands, admired for his disposition (Samson means "Sunny"), worshiped for his courage, honored for the position he held as a "Judge" in Israel and followed with undeviating devotion because of his superb military leadership. What a giant among men, and what a resounding tragedy when he goes down. "Weep ye fir trees," they cried, "for a cedar of Lebanon has fallen!"

And the same was true of Peter. He is one of the most exciting personalities of all time. Millions have felt a deep sense of kinship with him. There is much of Peter in all of us, and the warm human qualities of the man give us a regard for him that is different from our feeling for almost all of the others who people the pages of scripture.

There are two views to be taken of Peter. In one he is a despicable and spineless traitor who betrayed his divine Friend when danger crowded near. In the other view he is a very human disciple with all of the failings common to all men who went down when the going got rough. Whichever view you take remember before you cast any stones that the very things we condemn in Peter are our own sins. Who has not known moments of hotheaded impetuosity? Who has never vacillated in his devotion to his ideals? Who has never doubted the Divine purpose and has never denied his Lord by thought or word or action? Take care then, for whatever you hurl at Peter is likely to take on the nature of a boomerang.

With all of his faults—and they are many and bright-hued —Peter stands above them a giant for God, a great and thrilling man of action and color and excitement who stirs the imagination and demands one's respect. And when he goes down what a tragic day it is.

The strange thing in the story of these two giants is the fact that they did fall. There are few places in history where you will find such an utter about-face. Nowhere do you hear such loud protestations of fidelity and nowhere do you see such a speedy disintegration of purpose. But is it really so strange after all? One of the great dangers in being first is that you may be the first to fall. There are a great many who aspire to leadership, who would be the captains and lieutenants in the battle of life, who forget that in any war the greatest mortality rate is among captains and lieutenants.

Let us examine some of the reasons why these men failed. Was not one of the reasons self-confidence? Peter's experiences had given him an exalted idea of his own importance. In the flurry of excitement, in the growing crowds that followed Jesus, in the reflected glory he forgot that he would still have been a fisherman had it not been for the Master. He began to think of himself as "Peter, Second in Command to the

Prophet from Nazareth who was turning the world upside down." He was a person of importance. People questioned him about the Master. Scribes and Pharisees who had once scorned him now courted him seeking information. Then there was always that secretly-held vision of a Kingdom, and of himself on a throne—probably Throne Number Two. This new-born prominence blinded him to the fact that he had been a humble, poorly educated working man, an ill-smelling, horny-handed fisherman before Christ had called him.

It was the same with Samson. Such was his strength that he forgot his weakness. He gazed at the reflection of his physique, flexed his torso, bulged his biceps and forgot the source of his strength. He was too sure of himself. Afraid of temptation?—not he! Indeed, he welcomed it, and you have the incredible picture of the avowed and dedicated servant of God striding down into Gaza, into the very camp of the enemies of Israel, in brash and breath-taking self-assurance!

And they both went down. Of course they went down. They had grown arrogant. They had forgotten that humility is the foundation of character and that a life without it is as a house built upon the sand. So with us; the moment we begin to regard ourselves as superior, as adequate in ourselves, we are in danger. Pride is the fundamental sin and the father of every failure. "Let him that thinketh he standeth take heed lest he fall!"

Let all "successful" people reading these lines remember the lesson of these two men. It may be that you are unusually accomplished. You are gifted in a measure that sets you apart.

You are a leader in your field. You stand on a high rung on the ladder of life. Good, you are to be commended. But let us never forget the source of our success. Remember the words of the Apostle Paul, "Why are ye puffed up, for what hast thou that thou did'st not receive?" Your talent, your skills, your very life itself is a gift from God. You have developed your capacities, of course, and that is commendable, but let us remember that our every achievement would be impossible without the help of others and without the goodness of God. The greatest of men stand but a heartbeat from the grave. We must not blind ourselves to the fact that even as we have risen we may go down. How reads the ancient proverb?—"Pride goeth before destruction, and a haughty spirit before a fall." Then live with humility whatever your achievements for, "what hast thou that thou did'st not receive?"

Perhaps a word needs saying at this point to those who are members of the Church. Take care lest you fall into spiritual pride, lest you begin to look with hauteur upon those who are involved in gross sins and flagrant wrong. Watch lest you stand in judgment upon others for the standard by which you judge them will someday be applied to yourself. How easy it is to become one in spirit with the Pharisees; to belong to the Church, to observe religious practices, to say your prayers and yet to lack compassion for those who have not had your privileges. How stand you in judgment on another man's faith? How are you better than others when you are what you are simply through the unmerited goodness of God? Let us ever remember that we are at best "unprofitable servants." Samson forgot, Peter forgot, and it was the prelude to their downfall.

The second reason for the failure of these men was . . . bad company! Where does Samson seek his pleasure? In the company of Israel? No, in the camp of the enemy. See him standing there in Gaza, head and shoulders over the fawning crowd. Little wonder you soon see him shorn and impotent and badgered by these same people. Bad company!

And Peter? Who is that who stands warming himself at the fire of the hangers-on in the Temple courtyard? Who is that who consorts with the enemies of Jesus while the Master is facing his tormenters within? It is Peter! Peter of all people! Peter who had so recently taken the loyalty oath. Peter who had insisted that though all might forsake him he, Peter, would never fail. Little wonder there is a triple denial on his lips within the hour. Bad company!

It is not my purpose to deal here with the influence of friends and acquaintances upon our lives. We know how profound that influence may be. We recognize the truth in the dictum, "you can tell a man by the company he keeps." Our character is molded by our friends. How many young people have been drawn down the wrong road while running with the wrong crowd. The desire to go along with the crowd, the "herd instinct," frequently presses us into a conformity that does us hurt.

But there is another kind of bad company: the things that are our daily companions, the books we read, the magazines we devour, the television and radio programs to which we are addicted, the thoughts and ideas that dominate our mind. Who can doubt but what our lives are profoundly influenced by these daily companions of our leisure hours.

A concern about this is particularly pertinent because of the rash of harmful and utterly inane junk being purveyed in our generation. A flood of base and pornographic reading matter has broken through every moral dyke and has inundated every city and town in the nation. The average newsstand is an affront to every principle upon which the nation has been built. The noble doctrine of the freedom of the press has degenerated into a license to corrupt. Who can doubt that the lower moral standards and the increased delinquency of our day is not—at least in part—the harvest of the vapid and empty—and sometimes downright depraved—ideas that have been sown in our minds by these companions of our leisure? We fill our minds with a great deal of glorified nothing and fail to realize that slowly but certainly we are coloring our thinking, our ideals and our entire outlook. If it is true that "reading is vicarious living" then with what experiences do we identify ourselves in our reading? One is not, of course, calling for prudery or undue censorship but is suggesting that we would do well to contemplate the injury being dealt our nation, our communities, our homes, our youth and ourselves through . . . bad company!

Now to the final reason for the failure of these two mighty men. May it not be summed up in the word . . . sleep?

When is it that Samson is shorn? When is it that his Nazarite vows to God—the symbol of his strength—are

broken? It is while he sleeps. Behold the man of God asleep!
—on the lap of Delilah, asleep! Sleeping while Israel's future
hangs in the balance, sleeping while great and urgent tasks
lie unfinished. Where is the servant of God in this hour of
great need?—he is asleep!

And what was the doorstep of Peter's failure? It was the
sleep in the garden of Gethsemane. It seems incredible; this
is Jesus' greatest hour of trial and Peter lies asleep. One can
imagine that if he had been stirred into wakefulness he would
have murmured something about, "Oh leave me alone. I'm
tired. Dog-tired. I've followed until my feet are sore. I haven't
been getting my eight hours and I'm tired. Let me sleep . . ."
"Yes Peter, but Jesus is agonizing in the garden." "I know.
I know. He's done that a great many times before this, sometimes through the night, but I'm tired. Let me sleep."

Oh the dangers of spiritual sleep! The world in need and
we sleep! The world bleeding from a thousand wounds and
crying its need in a million voices and on we sleep. No
matter what our protestation of faith, no matter how high-
sounding our ideals, when the sufferings, the spiritual emptiness, the injustice and the inequities of our world fail to move
us and to awaken us, we are asleep and in great danger.

What of the Church today? Are we awake and busy at the
task? Are we meeting the unparalleled challenge of our
time with dedication and imagination, or are we asleep? One
fears that many of us are sunk in lassitude. With too many
it is "life as usual" in a world bursting at the seams. Ours

is a day that demands greatness and heroic resolve, and yet we sleep!

How quickly a people forget the lessons of the past. It was but a few years ago that Germany threatened the freedom of the world. Stabbed in wakefulness the allies arose and met the challenge. The enormity of the challenge and the sacrifice it demanded threw us back upon God. Recall the summons to prayer that went out with the announcement that D-Day had come. We were importuned to pray by president and senator, by king and prime minister, by archbishop and editor. Remember how the doors of the most ornate cathedral and the humblest mission hall hung open in invitation to pray and how, in the millions, we flocked in to seek the help of God.

Yet, though not many years have passed and though the wounds of war have not yet healed, most of us have lapsed back into the same careless somnolence of the prewar period. The soldier has forgotten his foxhole fervency, the sailor has forgotten his petition from the waves, the airman has forgotten the heavens above the one through which he flew, parents have forgotten the tear-stained pillow, the nation has forgotten her need. We sleep! In the midst of a world aflame we sleep! And as with Samson and Peter our sleep may preface our downfall.

But the saga of these two giants of the Bible is not all sung in the minor key. The heartening thing in their story is the fact that their failure was not final. Samson's was a pyrrhic victory but Peter came back to a life of rich usefulness. We rejoice in "the God of the second chance." Here is good counsel from these men. Live in humility in the service of the Creator. Beware of self-sufficiency, of bad company, of complacency. Let these giants speak to you who are strong and let their counsel be, "Let him that thinketh he standeth take heed lest he fall!"

Deep within us there seem to be two great and antipathetic tendencies. We aspire to do good but even as we do there is a downward pull. We are one in despair with the Apostle Paul when he cries, "I do not understand my own actions. For I do not do what I want, but I do the very thing I hate. I can will what is right but I cannot do it . . . wretched man that I am! Who will deliver me from this body of death?"

✿ 4 ✿

HOW TO BE GOOD THE EASY WAY

Perhaps you have read the couplet,

> Won't somebody give me some good advice
> On how to be naughty—and still be nice?

In a silly sort of way it sums up the attitude of millions today toward morality. We say, "I know I ought to be good, and to do what is right, and yet it's so much fun, at times, to be bad. I want a good conscience, a conscience that doesn't twinge me in the twilight of life, yet I want also to do what I please and to have what is popularly known as a good time." St. Augustine said it perfectly nearly sixteen hundred years ago when he prayed, "Lord, make me pure . . . but not yet!"

We have gotten so wrapped up in the achievement of success, in "getting ahead in the world," we have forgotten that character is the keynote to the good life and that there is no real happiness apart from goodness. Our standards are topsy-turvy. Our tendency is to put cleverness before goodness, success before sincerity and achievement before integrity. We honor without discrimination. A young lady said to a friend, "So-and-So is a great man; he speaks eight languages."

Her friend rather wisely replied, "Yes, he is a great man, but *not* because he speaks eight languages; he could be a liar in all eight!"

Now all of this brings us to the point: what is the purpose of religion—more specifically, the Christian religion? In plain, unmistakable English, avoiding theological terminology, *the purpose of the Christian religion is to make good people*— genuine, one-hundred-cents-on-the-dollar, transparently good people. Good, not simply in the avoidance of wrong, but good deep down on the inside in a natural kind of goodness that automatically overflows the life.

It would be almost impossible to think of a subject less likely to interest the average twentieth-century American. Goodness! If I were to speak of courage and relate the thrilling story of David Livingstone, or about peace of mind and tell you how to get it in ten easy lessons, or about success and suggest how you might get ahead in the world through prayer and Bible study, I think you would be interested. But who, today, is interested in such a pedestrian and prosaic virtue as "goodness"?

Say to the average young person today, "Don't you want to be holy?" and he will do one of two things: he will laugh in your face, or he will look at you incredulously and say, "Are you kidding?" "Blessed are the pure in heart? Blessed are those who hunger and thirst after goodness? Blessed are the meek? No! Blessed are the strong, the powerful, the people of wealth and influence. All the meek get for their pains today is to be shoved out of the way and stepped on by people who know what they want in life. Away with this milk-and-water, sentimental talk about goodness. It doesn't pay off. Not today."

Of course the trouble lies in the fact that we have become confused in our sense of values. The public flouting of moral standards in literature and entertainment has muddied our judgments until "goodness" seems a flat and pallid thing and "badness" is spicy and intriguing. The word "sin" has been dropped from our cultivated conversation. We don't like the sound of the word. We still use it, but with a different connotation. A perfume is called "My Sin." Sounds exciting, doesn't it? You register in an Ohio hotel and the clerk gives you a booklet listing the amusements of the city, entitled, *Where to Sin in Cincinnati.* You pass a theater marquee and the advertisement of the picture hints that all of the exciting things that happen to the star come about because of "her sin." It all sounds simply fascinating. The "bad" people are glamorous and exciting while the "good" people are insipid, pedestrian and dull.

As a consequence of this reversal of values millions of people have come to think of goodness as something that exists best in cloisters. "Goodness," you think, and immediately get a mental picture of black clothing, insipid quietness, long-faced sobriety, hands held just so, face furrowed in a frown of displeasure at anything that looks like fun and a life that is soft, prissy, sissified, inhibited, self-righteous and dull! Now if this is what Christian faith produces, then I say, "Away with it. I want nothing to do with it." But, in truth, this caricature is a million miles removed from what the Church means and the Bible means when it speaks of goodness.

One of the reasons goodness has fallen into such disrepute is the counterfeits that are passed off in its name. You know and I know there are some so-called "good people" who are just plain bores; the kind of people whose religion is feigned and unnatural, the kind you duck when you see them coming. You know the type; their lives are like Christmas trees, with all the ornaments tied on the outside for show, but the tree is dead and there is no real internal beauty. We have all met them, "the noble order of mote-removers and neighbor judgers," those self-appointed guardians of public morality, those everlasting inspectors of warts and carbuncles, with their noses always in other people's business and with free and unsought advice for all. From all such, dear Lord, deliver us!

I am not jesting. As the result of conversations with hundreds of men and women outside of the Church, the conviction has grown that the great enemy of genuine Christian goodness is not so much badness as it is the people who make goodness repugnant and drive thousands away from God and the Church, saying, "Well, if *that* is what religion produces, no thank you!"

But now the matter of genuine Christian goodness. First, let us remind ourselves that it isn't easy to be good. There is a sense, of course, in which goodness normally overflows the life lived in communion with God, but as anyone knows who has really tried it, it isn't easy to be good.

Life seems to be so conditioned that it is easier to do wrong than to do right. It is true in every area of living. It is easier to go down than to go up. It is easier to drift than to go against the current. It is easier to slip than to climb, to grow weeds than to grow flowers, to give in to temptation than to resist it.

More than that, people seem to make it difficult to be good. There is a tremendous, if subtle, pressure to make us conform to the norm. We are much concerned about public opinion. We do not want to appear "different," a misfit, a fanatic. We want to be a part of the gang, to "go along." As a consequence we often do things that we would not otherwise do. How many times we justify our actions by saying, "But *everybody* is doing it." There is an old saying, *"Vox populi, vox Dei"* (The voice of the people is the voice of God). It sounds good, but it is a lie.

The fact that "everybody" is doing something, that it is the accepted standard of behavior, does not mean that it is right. The fact that divorce is common does not necessarily mean that it is commendable. The fact that today's moral standards are lower does not mean that the lower standard is God's standard. The fact that much of today's literature is lewd and crude does not mean that it is good writing—even if it does sell a hundred thousand copies and is chosen as the selection of the month. The law of averages is not one of God's moral laws. The fact that certain standards are acceptable does not mean that they are right. There are some things in life that are not relative.

The mores of the crowd have been allowed to slip to the place where we have developed a new kind of hypocrite. The old-style hypocrite was a person who tried to appear better than he actually was. The new-style hypocrite tries to appear *worse* than he or she is.

Dining in a New York City restaurant recently I watched a young lady seated across the room. She was a beautiful girl, wholesome in appearance, about eighteen years old, and apparently waiting for someone who was to join her. She was wearing an extreme, off-the-shoulder black gown that seemed almost incongruous with her fresh youthfulness. She had ordered a cocktail and was sipping at it—doing her best to cover up the grimaces that the alcohol brought to her face—the while taking obviously inexperienced puffs on a cigarette in what she fondly believed was a sophisticated manner. I thought, "There is a girl doing her dead-level best to look *worse* than she is!"

There are millions like her. We have let the norm of public morality fall so low that millions of young people today do things, go along with things, become a part of things simply because they don't want to seem slow or "square" or unsophisticated. Many a person living in conformity with today's norm is living far below his personal standard. The pressure is terrific. Nobody wants to seem "different" so we go along with the crowd. As a consequence we have developed a new kind of hypocrite: the person who tries to appear *worse* than he or she is—and it is an American tragedy!

But now to return to this matter of goodness. Let it be clear that mere negative goodness is not enough. Many think it is. Many think that a person is Christian because he guards his life against wrong; that he is good because he has forsworn certain gross misdeeds. There are people, often sincere and well-intentioned, whose greatest concern is to prune things from their lives. This may or may not be desirable but it is certainly not Christianity.

It is an interesting fact that the words "holiness" and "health" derive from the same root. An overconcern about one's health is called a phobia. Similarly, an overconcern about one's soul is abnormal Christianity. How does one go about being healthy? Certainly not by worrying about illness all the time. You do not find health by washing your hands every hour on the hour, or by wearing a gauze mask during conversations, or by gargling after every encounter, or by carrying a portable sterilizing kit when eating out. Of course not. Health comes when you cease being preoccupied over germs and begin to observe the laws of health; getting enough rest, good food, exercise and recreation. Similarly, spiritual health comes when you cease to be preoccupied with yourself and, observing certain daily spiritual disciplines, lose your life in the service of God and others.

Christianity is not a matter of making a vow to be better. There is an utterly wrong impression abroad that religion has to do with clenched fists, a set jaw, a furrowed brow and deep resolves. Millions of people erroneously think it is all a matter of making new resolutions, turning over a new leaf, taking a pledge or swearing a vow. But this way will not work. We have tried it and it doesn't work. Every New Year's Day we try again, or at the communion service, or whenever we see our actions are hurting someone we love or endangering our future. We have tried it, and it doesn't work. It not only will not work, it is not the gospel. The word "gospel" means "good news," and there is no good news in telling a man wrestling with his baser self that what he needs to do is to try harder. That is adding burdens rather than lifting them.

"Try harder!" Do you think that was the message that brought thousands crowding around Jesus when he was here on earth? Do you believe, even for a moment, that this was all he had to say to Mary Magdalene when she looked up at him with tears on her face and a black blanket of guilt on her heart? Can you believe that he merely looked at her and said, "Try harder, Mary?" Was this his message of hope for the hopeless? Was this the reason they crowded round him in the thousands? Is this the message that has kept the church alive through the centuries? Say "try harder" to Mary Magdalene and she would have looked at you with shriveling scorn in her eyes. Say "try harder" to that cynical publican, Matthew, and he would have jeered at you in derision. Say "try harder" to the dying thief on the cross and he would have turned his pain-contorted face away to die hopelessly.

If the gospel merely means trying harder to be better, making new resolutions, summoning up inner strength, it means this—let's face it—it means that God cannot save you and that it is up to you to save yourself by your own will power. And you have been trying that for years now and your life is far from what you know it ought to be.

How then do you live the good life, the life pleasing to God? The answer is a simple one, a deceptively simple one: by living your life as it was intended to be lived, in a daily relationship with God. Our trouble is that we have forgotten we are creatures and that, even as our lives have come from God, we are incomplete apart from Him. The reason for the confusion, the frustration, the aimlessness and emptiness of our lives is that we have left God out. Just as a car is designed to run on gasoline and will not operate properly with any other fuel, so our lives are made to be lived with God and are bound to go awry when we separate ourselves from Him to go our own way.

How long will it be before we realize that the universe did not just happen? There is a purpose at the heart of life. Life is to be lived a certain way and "The Way" is revealed to us in history and, perfectly, in Jesus Christ. How long will our world go its own way and then wonder why it is embroiled in near-constant war and filled with tragedy and heartbreak?

A prominent man was being interviewed by a newspaper reporter. The reporter said, "I understand, sir, that you are a self-made man." The man turned to the reporter and said slowly, "Yes, I guess I am what you would call a self-made man." Then he added ruefully, "But if I had it to do over again I think I'd call in a little help." It is precisely because we have lived life our own way that we are frustrated and empty. In the ancient words, "All we, like sheep, have gone astray. We have turned, every one *to his own way.* . . ." And our own way has led to three wars in a generation, to economic chaos in half of the world, to starvation in the midst of surplus, to the possibility of total destruction and to a frantic sense of lostness. We listened to Jesus and dismissed his words with, "It's all so idealistic and impractical. Jesus is such a visionary. His ideas are lovely but they just won't work in this tough old world." Well, I wonder! Look around you and see what our hardheaded, realistic, down-to-earth approach has brought us to. We stand on the edge of an abyss from which there may be no drawing back. Maybe the idealistic Jesus wasn't so impractical after all. Maybe our "down-to-earth" ways need the touch of heaven before they drag us down to total destruction.

Our world problems are but the extension of our personal problems. Our world will not be better until we are. Then how may we find this inner goodness without which our civilization is doomed? The Greeks had a phrase, "Know thyself." May we not make it read, "Know thyselves," for are we not complex and many-sided personalities? Edward Sanford Martin puts it,

> Within my earthly temple there's a crowd;
> There's one of us that's humble, one that's proud,
> There's one that's broken-hearted for his sins,
> There's one that unrepentant sits and grins;

There's one that loves his neighbor as himself,
And one who cares for naught but fame and pelf.
From much corroding care I should be free
If I could once determine which is me.

Deep within us there seem to be two great and antipathetic tendencies. We aspire to do good but even as we do there is a downward pull. We are one in despair with the Apostle Paul when he cries, "I do not understand my own actions. For I do not do what I want, but I do the very thing I hate. . . . I can will what is right, but I cannot do it. . . . Wretched man that I am! Who will deliver me from this body of death."

There is a tug-of-war within the soul. We seek to do good and find our best resolves defeated. We stretch every nerve in a struggle for goodness only to be bested by our baser nature again and again. What's to be done? How may life move upward rather than ever up and down? In our own unaided strength the course of battle flows and ebbs as the tide. There is no winning it in our own strength. We must have help.

"Our help is in the Lord," cries the Psalmist, and He is at hand. Jesus said, "Behold, I stand at the door and knock; if any one hears my voice and opens the door (opens up his life to God), I will come in." If we will but grant Him the lordship of our life: in the everlasting tug-of-war within us He will throw His strength on the side of right and give us the ability to be what we want to be and what He asks us to be.

How may you be good the easy way?—by getting some help. By ending the solitary struggle for goodness in which you have been unsuccessfully engaged for years and by opening up your life to God's wisdom and His strength.

Faith is not a faint hope all shored up with logic and syllogism. Men find that no matter what they may say in moments of security they believe in God in foxholes, or when the baby is being rushed to the hospital, or when death stands stark and staring before their eyes. Yes, there is a God, and deep within us we know it, know it despite the fog of doubt that sometimes shuts Him from our sight.

❧ 5 ❧

LAND OF BEGINNING AGAIN

ONE would be presumptuous indeed who would claim fully to understand God. "His ways are past finding out." We peer through telescopes and microscopes into ever-increasing mystery. It is impossible to stretch the mind until we can comprehend the immensity of space or to narrow the focus of our vision until we can glimpse the infinitely minute building blocks of which our world is compounded. Every new answer gives birth to a dozen new problems. Following the path that leads into the deepening mysteries of the universe we find its branches innumerable and its turnings unpredictable.

So it is with Jesus; he is utterly unpredictable. He invariably does the unexpected. You expect heavenly royalty to be born in a palace but he comes to a stable. You imagine he will select as his immediate disciples the scholars of his time but he calls fishermen and taxgatherers and the like, and out of this common clay fashions the foundation for his Kingdom. You expect him to hold converse with men of comparable knowledge but he is discovered one day in animated conversation with an illiterate woman known to have had some five husbands. As his patrons you expect him

67

to select the society leaders of his day but he chooses an obscure pair of sisters from the little town of Bethany and a woman from the shadows called Mary Magdalene. You expect him to triumph over his enemies but when they are done with him they have nailed him to the rough wood of a Roman cross.

It was so with his teaching. He was full of paradox, Would you save your life? he asks—then "lose it." Don't hate your enemies, love them. Pray for those who do you hurt. When your right cheek is smitten, turn the other. When you are persecuted as one of his followers, leap and jump for joy for you are in good company. Are you poor, are you in mourning, are you being slandered?—"Blessed art thou!" Don't seek to dominate, seek to serve. Eventually, the last shall be first and the first shall be last. Who ever heard such teaching! This Jesus is utterly unpredictable.

This is the thought that badgers the preacher when he would try to explain God's dealing with men. You hearken back to the experiences of the great saints, you observe the ways in which God has worked in history, you study the life and teaching of Jesus and then, just when you have things all worked out and a "plan of salvation" neatly packaged, you suddenly come upon the unpredictable and all your neat little categories fall apart.

This is the danger of all authoritarian religion; it tries to press God into a mold. It presumes that God is bound to act as experience would indicate He has acted in the past. It would bind the Almighty with the cords of human limita-

tion. It forgets that God deals with us as children and not as
things. He loves men as a father loves his children; equally
and yet differently. They asked the mother of five boys which
she loved best and she answered, "The one who is away until
he returns, and the one who is sick until he is well." No two
individuals are identical and our Father deals with no two
of us identically. The unpredictable God will not fit into our
little categories.

Consequently, any attempt to explain the meaning of the
Gospel is bound, by the nature of things, to fall short. Not
even Jesus can fully explain the mystery of God's purposes.
When he was on earth he tried to convey it to his disciples
but finite minds cannot grasp the infinite so he taught with
analogies and parables and pictures. "It is like this," he would
say, "and this . . . and this." It is like the coming and the
going of the wind. You hear the wind and you see its effect
in the clouds scudding across the sky and the whirlpools of
dust on the road, but "you do not know whence it comes or
whither it goes." You do not know its origin or its end, but
you know it exists because you can see the results of it round
about you.

So it is with the *modus operandi* of the Gospel; you do not
know where it comes from other than the great heart of God
(and where is that?), you do not know what it comes to
other than the heart of a man (and that is but a figure of
speech), but though you cannot analyze it you know it exists
because you can see the results of it in the lives of thousands
of men and women across the centuries.

Consequently, if you press for an answer as to how the Gospel operates in human life, the answer must be, "I don't know." This is not to say that Christian faith is presumption. There is a Christian philosophy that, granted your original premise, is as valid as any philosophy. In the realm of psychology you can point out certain spiritual "laws" apparently operative. You can explain and illustrate, you can quote learned men and enter into prolonged discussion, but when you have finished you will not fully and satisfactorily have accounted for it. In the last analysis the preacher must present the evidence to be seen in the transformed lives of people, lift up your eyes to God, and say to you, "Taste and see that God is good."

But now to the question, "What is the Gospel?" Let us begin negatively by disabusing our mind of many common misconceptions. First, *the Gospel is not bad news*. Translated, the word "gospel" means, simply, "good news." Too frequently it has been made to resemble something much more like bad news. Too often it has been preached as a narrow and inhibiting code of "thou shalt nots" and millions have looked at this forbidding, crepe-hung thing and have turned away. Too often the Gospel has been presented as the observing of certain ordinances—you must be baptized, you must take communion, you must join the Church, you must observe this or that ecclesiastical edict. These matters are of great significance and vast importance but they are not the Gospel. Indeed, they are tedious and tiresome duties unless a man has first found a meaningful faith. Helpful and essential as they may be after the life with God has begun, they are tasks to be endured before. The Gospel is not a burden for the back but wings for the soul. It is not bad news.

Moreover, *the Gospel is not what is commonly regarded as orthodoxy*. As was hinted above there is no inviolable pattern by which men come to God. Our traditional ways of doing things, our forms and our worship are not sacrosanct. There is no single road that leads to God and of which any group or individual is custodian. Not everyone comes to a "mourners' bench." Not everyone has an overwhelming emotional experience. Not everyone can put his finger on a date on a calendar and say, "Then it was that I found God." Not everyone has an identical experience with God, nor has everyone the same measure of assurance. We in the Church must take care that we do not set up arbitrary standards and hold men at arm's length unless they have come up the same road we traveled.

The record in the Bible makes it clear that no two people came to Jesus in the same way. Peter came after a discouraging night of fishing. Zacchaeus came through curiosity. The thief on the cross came in the sobering shadow of death. Paul came as a devout and zealous churchman, Mary Magdalene came filled with self-loathing. They were different personalities, they reacted to different situations in different ways but—and this is the point—they came to the same Christ and found the answers to their diversified needs in him.

Further, *the Gospel is not the faith of the ignorant*. For a considerable period in recent history a scientific age scorned the Gospel as "Infantile!" Superior wisdom smiled in a con-

descending way at "this collection of archaic myths and mystical tommyrot" and tossed the ancient creeds on the ash heap,
and our wise old world, our shiny, "brave new world," the
practical, realistic "world of tomorrow" went its own way.
Then suddenly we were engulfed in another war, a war that
took twenty million casualties, a war that suddenly funneled
upward into an ominous mushroom-shaped cloud. Suddenly
we had an atomic bomb in one hand and a hydrogen bomb
in the other and a cobalt bomb in the blueprints and annihila-
tion staring us in the face. Then men everywhere—presidents,
scientists, economists, historians and philosophers—were crying with one voice, "We must rediscover the spiritual realities
or we are lost! We must find a vital faith. Except we repent
we shall all likewise perish." Suddenly we began to see that
the "foolishness of God" is the ultimate wisdom.

While the Gospel is not the faith of the ignorant, it is a
simple faith. And this is where men stumble. Depend only
upon your reason and you will miss it. God is known by faith,
and while faith never contradicts reason it does transcend it.
This does not mean that the Gospel is irrational. Faith is not
credulity. You do not leave your intellect in the narthex when
you go to church. Jesus said that we are to worship God "with
the whole mind," and to fail to think is to sin against Him
who created the intellect.

Too frequently belief in God has been presented as belief
despite the evidence. But Christian faith is not an unscientific
credulity, it is not flying in the face of facts, it is not shutting
the eyes to reality. It is not as in *Alice in Wonderland* where

Alice asks the Queen how old she is and the Queen answers, "One hundred and one, five months and a day." Alice says, "Oh I can't believe that!" The Queen says, "You can't? Then shut your eyes, take a deep breath and try again."

The Gospel is simple, but we must not be misled at this point. Did you ever try to make a "simple" Parisian gown? Have you ever tried to paint a picture as "simple" as the "Mona Lisa?" Have you realized that the entire universe, with all its variety and complexity, is made of less than one hundred basic elements? Simple? Yes, but profound beyond the furthest reaches of imagination. The Gospel, while simple, is not the faith of the ignorant.

But enough of the negative. What, positively, is the Gospel? As was hinted a moment ago, the word "gospel" means "good news." Now here is something all can understand. We all know what news is. We are all interested in the news. I know some people who can hardly wait to repeat it when they get hold of a particularly juicy morsel of news. I have met men and women who would, I think, be ready to die if they could be the first to break the news to their friends.

But you will remember that the Gospel is not merely news, it is *good* news, and good news is a rare thing in our troubled world. Listen to the radio, scan the pages of the newspaper, look about you at your friends; we live in a world filled with bad news. Every long-distance telephone call starts the heart to beating. Every unexpected telegram fills with a vague foreboding. Go into the public clinic of any major hospital in any large city and glimpse the distilled misery that is there. Go into the heart of any slum. Go into the sleazy little bars and night clubs. Go into the jails and police courts, into the divorce courts, the mental hospitals, the funeral parlors . . . ! Go anywhere. Bad news! The world is full of it.

Into this world of bad news Christ comes, and his message is the Gospel . . . *good news*. The angel heralded it across the hills outside Bethlehem, "Behold, I bring you good news of a great joy which will come to all the people!" It is good news for everyone; for the good and the bad, for the strong and the helpless, for the moral and the sinful; good news to those who suffer, to those who are in despair, to those who are confused and lost. With all else the Gospel may be it is first and foremost good news.

More specifically it is the good news that there is a God and that He is concerned about men. The Bible doesn't try to prove God, it takes Him for granted. The first words of the first book are, "In the beginning, God. . . ." The Bible doesn't try to prove God for, in the last analysis, do we ever really believe that He does not exist? One would not suggest that we do not know moments and years of doubt; awful, soul-shaking, ultimate doubt. Even such a resolute believer as Martin Luther cried out, "Who has not known that awakening of a dark morning covered by the black blanket of the last ultimate doubt?" Even Jesus knew the meaning of doubt—was he not "tempted in all points like as we are"? The Bible proceeds on the assumption that believing in God is instinctive. Faith is not a faint hope all shored up with logic or syllogism. Men find that no matter what they may say in moments of security they believe in God in foxholes, or when the baby is being rushed to the hospital, or when death stands stark and staring before their eyes. Yes, there is a God, and deep within us we know it, know it despite the fog of doubt that sometimes shuts Him from our sight.

But the fact that God exists is not good news. Some of the gods of history have been cruel and capricious and only placated with some costly sacrifice. But the God revealed in the Gospel, though inflexible in His justice and austere in His demands, is a God of love. This is no dispassionate deity, standing apart from our world and its problems. The God of the Gospel is a God of love, a "Father in Heaven," a God who loved so much He entered into human experience: to be "tempted in all points like as we are," to be "crucified, dead and buried," to become "a Comforter," a "Friend that sticketh closer than a brother," an "ever-present help in time of trouble." The God of the Gospel is Jesus Christ, "Emmanuel" (God with us), helping, guiding, enlightening, empowering . . . redeeming! And this is good news!

Notice further that the Gospel is the good news there is a land of beginning again. Who among us would not, if we could, live part of our life over again? Who would not like to change some things, to rectify certain mistakes, to take back hasty, cutting words, to live certain hours over again differently? We are all haunted by the specter of misspent hours. A soldier confessed to a chaplain, "To be honest, Padre, I was glad when the war came and I was called up. It enabled me to draw a line across my life and start again."

Imagine, if you can, how thrilling it would be if someone

were to come to you with the power to undo the past, if someone were to announce to you that there is "a land of beginning
again." If there was offered to you the opportunity to start
life afresh, would you not thrill to it? Well, this is, in effect,
precisely what the Gospel proclaims: the good news that there
is a land of beginning again, that with all of our false starts
God will grant us yet another chance to make something
worth while out of life.

This is the wonder of God's forgiveness as it is heralded
in the Christian Gospel. It frees a man from his past and sets
him on the road to worth-while living. Millions of men and
women live under a gray cloud of guilt. What a grievous thing
is guilt; it stunts ambition, debilitates energy, encumbers the
mind, distorts the personality and even causes the guilty to
seek failure and pain. To such as these Jesus comes with the
glad, good news of forgiveness. Across every century men
have heard the words, "Thy sins be forgiven thee. Go and
sin no more," and, like Pilgrim, their burden has fallen away
and they have stood afresh at the gates of life. In his book
Psychology, Religion and Healing, . . . Dr. Leslie D. Weather-
head says, "The forgiveness of God, in my opinion, is the
most powerful therapeutic idea in the world." Dr. James S.
Stewart says, "Who can tell the incalculable results of the
word of absolution for the integration of human personalities?"

But the good news of forgiveness does not mean the past
has ceased to be.

> The Moving Finger writes; and, having writ,
> Moves on: nor all your Piety nor Wit

Shall lure it back to cancel half a Line,
Nor all your Tears wash out a Word of it.

The Prodigal is forgiven but the joy that came in the assurance of his father's love did not blot out the memory that he had been in "the far country." Nor did it undo the consequences of his failure. It is said that on the morning after his return home, the Prodigal arose late, fatigued by the long journey home and the late night of celebration, and going out into the bright sunlight of the field where his father was working, saw for the first time that *his father's hair had turned white!* Our failures leave their mark and even tears of repentance cannot wash them away.

But though the past cannot be undone, we can be freed from its weight and move out to begin again. The Prodigal cannot undo or forget the past but he can find forgiveness for the past and a fresh start, surrounded by his father's love and strengthened by his father's resources.

And so may we. We too may stand at "the gates of the new life." To which of us does this not come as good news? Standing among our broken vows, our shattered dreams and our messed-up lives, who among us does not need a second chance?

Then, even as we stand, God comes, compassionate and speaking of beginning again. Not as before in our weakness, but in His strength. Not pointlessly, but now with a new purpose. Not groping into increasing darkness, but following a Light that grows brighter with each day. This is "the Gospel of a second chance" . . . and it is good news!

Let's stop making prayer profound, theological and subject to traditional patterns. Prayer is the normal relationship between a child and its Father—you being the child and God being your Heavenly Father. There are no special phrases without which Heaven is barred to us. Surely God is no petty, insecure tyrant insisting on some divine protocol.

6

LIFE LOOKS UP

MAY a modern man pray? With the changes in our world view that have been occasioned by the increase of knowledge in recent decades, may an informed person pray? Is the simple, uncomplicated faith of other generations possible or even desirable today?

I lunched recently with a friend, a university student, immediately following a service in which I had spoken about prayer. In the midst of the meal he suddenly leaned across the table and with a trace of impatience in his voice asked, "Why should I bother to pray? Didn't Jesus himself say that God knows what we need before we ask Him? How dare we presume to ask God to do our will in a universe apparently controlled by immutable law? And more than that, do you think it is intellectually healthy to run to God with all your problems and to slough off on Him responsibilities that ought to be faced up to? Isn't it a fact that prayer is simply a form of escape from reality? Why," he asked, "should I bother to pray?"

These are questions that most thoughtful people have put to themselves, and because, at first glance, the questions seem to argue that prayer is presumptuous, irrational and even injurious many a modern has come to doubt the validity of prayer.

It is, nevertheless, a fact that most Americans pray. A poll has yielded the information that 96 per cent of all Americans believe in God and there can be little doubt but what at some time or another most if not all of these pray. The will to pray is almost instinctive. We may fail to pray when life is serene but when troubles pyramid themselves upon us and we come to the end of our tether, we pray. It has even been said that

> When the Devil is sick
> The Devil a saint would be.

But most of our prayers are spasmodic and occasional. We pray in church, for five minutes at the fag-end of the day, at mealtime, or desperately, urgently in time of crisis. Few people have been able to make prayer the vital source of insight and power it is designed to be, and the likelihood is that with most of us prayer will remain an irregular, untrained, spasmodic thing; a fruitless, half-superstition "for emergency use only."

Let us begin with an attempt to understand why prayer is so meaningless to so many. Is it not because we seem to get along very well without it? Some time in the past we prayed and nothing seemed to happen. At another time, over a long period, we did not pray and everything went along smoothly. It did not make any apparent difference whether we did or whether we didn't. We rather imagined that if there was any-

thing to this business of prayer it ought to have clearly defined ramifications in daily life. We were somewhat like
the little girl who said, "We haven't said grace at our house
for a month now and nothing has happened . . . yet." So
often we have prayed and asked God for something and
there seemed to be no answer. Because there seemed to be
no answer we took the next step and began, perhaps uncon-
sciously, to wonder whether there was anyone *to* answer.
And if there is no God, why pray?

But prayer is not a mechanism by which we get an immediate and automatic response from the deity. You cannot,
as in the automat, put in a nickel's worth of prayer and
automatically receive a nickel's worth of blessing. Indeed,
have you ever paused to think what would happen if all our
prayers *were* answered affirmatively? What chaos and discord
there would be in the universe if it was controlled by the
whim of anyone who bent his knee! What would happen in
wartime when equally virtuous people on both sides prayed for
victory? If all of our prayers were answered affirmatively it
would simply mean that God had abdicated and that we were
running the universe. We have made such a notable failure
in running our world and our own lives that one shudders to
think of the consequences if we controlled the universe.

You see, piety is no guarantee of wisdom. The mere act
of prayer does not perfect one's judgment. You may petition
fervently and yet foolishly. In the words of the Apostle James,
"Ye receive not, because ye ask amiss."

It is precisely because God is "our Father" that some of our prayers are answered negatively. This does not mean the prayer was not answered; in point of fact it was—the answer was "No." No father worthy of the name would grant all of his children's requests. An infant, in ignorance, might reach out a dimpled hand for a shiny razor blade and cry when it is denied. The father says "No" to the child because he loves the child. So our Heavenly Father sometimes denies us things we want because He loves us too much to say "Yes."

But now to some positive suggestions. How may the person who prays only occasionally, or the person who finds prayer a foreign and unnatural experience, learn to pray in a natural and significant way?

1. You must believe in God. There is a sentence in the Bible: "Whoever would draw near to God must believe that he exists and that he rewards those who seek him." It is not necessary to hold a particular concept of God but prayer apart from a belief in a compassionate deity is not only unlikely but its practice would be at best a mere psychological exercise hardly described by the term "prayer."

Do not postpone prayer until you have your views about God all worked out. It is *in* praying that you learn about God. God is not known through logic but by experience. We tend to say, "Show me and I'll believe." God says, "Believe and I will show you." It is possible to know a great many facts concerning God and yet fail to know Him in experience— like the theologian who was so busy arguing the fact of God he forgot to say his prayers.

If you believe in God and yet your concept of God is

so hazy you do not know where to begin, begin with silent prayer or meditation. The Bible says, "Be still, and know that I am God." Go apart somewhere where there is no distraction and begin to think about the meaning back of life. If possible sit so there is some distant vista before you; sit at the water's edge, or on a hilltop, or looking up at the stars. If this is not possible, sit in a darkened room or in a church, or simply close your eyes. If you find it helpful to kneel or to recline, do so. Posture is unimportant so long as you are not distracted by discomfort.

You will find that your mind will wander. This is normal. Bring your thoughts back to the purpose at hand. Do not merely empty your mind, think about a specific idea. Ask yourself, for instance, how can there be such an apparently ordered universe if there is no God behind it? How can I account for the fragile loveliness of these flowers, of that sunset, or for the goodness I see in some of the people I know if these things do not have their origin in God? If there is no God what are the alternatives? Am I content with the explanation that all of this "just happened," that it is the result of "the coincidental collocation of atoms?"

After a few periods of silent meditation you may be able to shake off what might be called your "cosmic shyness" and begin to pray aloud. Even if you can only manage, "God help me to understand . . ." at least make a start. Prayer, like so many other things, comes easier with practice. Begin in silence; the greatest saints have found God there.

2. Get rid of the idea that prayer is primarily a way of

getting things from God. Many never pray except to ask—like the boy who was asked if he prayed every night and who answered, "No, not every night, because there's some nights when I don't want nothin'." Such an immature attitude toward prayer turns a holy thing into an instrument of selfishness and seeks to use God as a kind of cosmic errand boy.

Prayer is not an attempt to get what we want but to give God an opportunity to do what He wants. It is not begging from God but co-operation with Him. The thing to be sought in prayer is the will of God. We do not seek to change God's mind (were that possible) and to persuade Him to do what He does not intend to do. It is not to change God but to change ourselves and our world that we pray. It is not, "Thy will be *changed*," but always "Thy will be *done*."

Too often we think of prayer as a groping after God when in reality it is the opening up of our life to Him. We, in seeking God, should realize that it is He who is seeking us, and that prayer is one of the ways in which we come to know and understand Him. We have reversed the parable of the Lost Sheep. We act as though the Shepherd is lost and the sheep are doing the seeking. We speak of "finding God" but God is not lost—we are! Finding God is a matter of letting Him find us, and how often we are found of Him in prayer.

3. Realize that prayer is, essentially, a simple thing and that it takes no special skill. Too long has prayer been regarded as a complex, mystical, otherworldly something whose richest rewards are reserved for the ministry or the initiated. We

need to strip this cover of unreality from prayer. It is not difficult to understand. Prayer is so simple it may be defined in a sentence: *It is the normal relationship between a child and its father—you being the child and God being your Heavenly Father!* Prayer is simply talking to your Father.

I saw this exemplified in a visit with a friend, the father of four children. During the course of our rather extended conversation all four children came to him for one reason or another. The first, a small boy, came in to ask, "Daddy, may I have a nickel for an ice cream cone?" Later a girl of about seven came hobbling in in tears. She had barked her shinbone while playing and wanted her father to "kiss the pain away." He did, and the most astonishing instance of instantaneous healing took place. The third child, a girl in her teens, appeared with a homework problem she could not solve. He did not give her the answer but showed her how to find it. The fourth, his youngest, came in and climbed up onto his lap and settled down. He looked down at the boy and said, "What do you want, dear? Can't you see that Daddy is busy?" The child answered, "Oh, I didn't want anything. I just wanted to be with you."

What a near-perfect analogy to prayer. Prayer is the child (you) coming to your Father (in Heaven): for the things you need, or when you have bumped your shinbone on some rough place in life and want your Father to—so to speak—"kiss the pain away," or when you face problems you cannot solve in your own wisdom and seek, not the answer but the wisdom to find the answer, or, most important, not to ask anything, but simply to come into His presence because you love Him.

Let's stop making prayer profound, theological and subject to traditional patterns. Prayer is the normal relationship between a child and its Father—you being the child and God being your Heavenly Father. There are no special phrases without which Heaven is barred to us. Surely God is no petty, insecure tyrant insisting on some divine protocol. It has been said, "God hears the stammered prayer of the child more readily than the printed prayer of the Bishop." While there are ramifications to prayer that the wisest man cannot plumb, prayer is, essentially, a simple thing and we must not complicate it.

4. Prayer is not a matter of proper posture. A great many feel that prayer may only be made when one has bowed the head or kneeled down or assumed some position traditionally connected with prayer. These postures have proven helpful to millions across centuries but they are not sacrosanct. It is an interesting fact that in the record of the four Gospels there is only one instance where Jesus *kneeled* to pray. One is not arguing from silence to contend that he did not commonly kneel to pray but where reference is made to his posture it is usually stated that he stood with eyes open and lifted heavenward. This freedom from pattern is to be seen in the lives of other great men and women in the Bible: they prayed kneeling, seated, standing, prostrate, walking in the field, in prison, in bed, in the market place . . . even on a cross!

There are as many individual ways of praying as there are

individuals. It is your attitude that is important and not your posture. If you find it unnatural to pray in the traditional manner, experiment until you find the way best suited to your needs.

A minister of national prominence goes into his study and paces back and forth, talking out his problems with God. A housewife pauses in the kitchen, throws her apron up over her head and, under its canopy, prays. Another woman, the first tasks of the day accomplished, goes into the living room, seats herself in an easy chair, puts her head back, crosses her hands on her lap and prays. A businessman walks out into the garden and standing beneath the starry heavens, prays. A teenage girl slips into an open church near by and sits silently in a pew. Find the way best suited to you. It is your attitude that is important and not your posture.

Begin by putting a "parenthesis of prayer" around your day. Begin and end the day with God. When you awaken do not immediately get out of bed. Lie there for a moment and pray something like this, "Father, I stand on the verge of another day. I do not know what today will bring; perhaps trouble or tragedy or happiness. Father, I give this day to Thee. Go before me and go with me into it and help me to live this day for Thee." In the pressure of responsibility you may forget the actual prayer but He to whom you gave the day will not forget you. Just as you forget your breakfast but your breakfast does not forget you but gives you strength for the morning, so the God to whom you dedicated the day will be with you in it. At the end of the day, before you sleep, pray again. In your own words pray after this fashion, "Father, I thank Thee for having been with me today. I thank Thee for the strength Thou did'st give me to face that crisis. Forgive me for the places where I failed. And now grant me rest in sleep that I may live tomorrow as Thou wouldst have me do." Put a parenthesis of prayer around your day; begin and end it with God. It can make all the difference in the world.

5. Realize that prayer does not necessarily have to be articulated. The Apostle Paul bade the members of the church at Thessalonica to "pray without ceasing." Someone might comment rather testily, "Isn't that typical of the impracticality of religion. How does a person immersed in life pray without ceasing?"

In a mystery that none can fully explain His spirit dwells within us. In the words of Moses, "In him we live and move and have our being."

> Closer is He than breathing,
> And nearer than hands and feet.

We must not think of Him as resident in a distant heaven and near us only when we pray. We must realize that in every experience of life He is with us, not on occasion but always. When this has been realized we are ready to begin to obey the suggestion to "pray without ceasing."

Begin in this way; in the midst of your daily duties turn your thoughts to God. Your hands may be busy at some task, your eyes may be open, your lips may not move and yet you are "talking" to God.

Prayer is the soul's sincere desire,
Uttered or unexpressed. . . .

You can pray while dusting or doing the dishes, while driving the car, while walking down the street, while mingling with a crowd. A secretary "talks" to God in the few seconds it takes to place a new sheet of paper in the typewriter and make the automatic adjustments of the sheet to prepare it for typing. A businessman prays while waiting for the stop light to turn green. A football player prays between plays—not to win but to do his best. The prayer may not be articulated, there may be no visible indication that prayer is being offered, but the life is reaching out to God. When we have learned this we will know we may pray *anywhere* and that busy people can "pray without ceasing."

6. Realize that prayer is blasphemy if it does not alter your life. We must not delude ourselves that our prayers are the words we utter when we pray. Our real prayers are the desires that dominate our lives. It is easy to prime the pump and have the words gush out in a torrent of pious phrases, but the proof of what we really want is to be seen in the way we live. You are better not to pray at all than to pray for one thing and seek another. It is wrong to pray for peace and then do nothing to achieve it. It is wrong to pray for the Church and not support it. It is wrong to pray for strength to defeat an improper desire and then put yourself in the place of temptation.

What we really want is clearly revealed in the way we live. Our true prayers are the desires that dominate our lives.

To paraphrase Emerson, "What we are speaks so loudly that God cannot hear what we say."

Begin then to learn to pray. Do not let another day pass but that you reach out to God. Draw aside from the frantic turbulence of the world round about you and in the silence pray the prayer of Jesus' disciples, "Lord, teach me to pray."

Whenever men look about for the perfect life, the radiant, joyful life, the truly happy life, they turn to Jesus. And yet his life led to a cross. How strange! Stranger still is the fact that those who serve only themselves, who pamper their every whim and grant license to their every appetite, are the barren and unhappy ones.

7

LIFE CAN BE BEAUTIFUL—IF

WHAT does the average person want from life? If the question were put, the answer would probably be, "I want to find happiness." There might be some who, in a fine show of bravado, would claim their goals are above and beyond this, but if we get down to the deep underlying motives, most of us do what we do in the hope of finding that sense of fulfillment and well-being described by the word "happiness." The Founding Fathers struck a deep chord when they recognized as one of man's inalienable rights the right to "the pursuit of happiness."

There is plenty of evidence to indicate how deep-seated this desire is. It can be seen in the hundreds of recipes for happiness being peddled on every hand. Most of them tell you how to get things from life; how to be successful, how to win friends, how to be popular and attractive, how to make money. The reading habits of our generation further reveal a deep need for inner peace and serenity and a seeking for answers in psychiatry and religion. The entertainment business has become the third largest industry as millions seek escape and amusement in a ceaseless round of activity. The pursuit of happiness is indeed fundamental to life.

But have you noticed this: though millions of people are seeking happiness few seem to find it. Ask yourself how many of your immediate acquaintances would you describe as truly happy—using the word in its full sense. How many of the marriages you know of would you describe as things of beauty and mutual helpfulness. What of yourself?

Our difficulty consists in that we are confused about the nature of happiness. We make a fundamental mistake in our approach to life. We live under the illusion that if only we get certain things—money, prestige, fame, power, any of a thousand things—that somehow these things will bring with them that deep-down sense of satisfaction we feel life ought to give. But there is a peculiar paradox here, for some of the people who have all of these things seem peculiarly unhappy. Indeed, some of the wealthiest and best-known people in the world are among the most miserable.

Some years ago I was sitting in my automobile listening to a news broadcast and waiting for my wife who was shopping —something I do not infrequently, in company with all husbands. The announcer reported that a famous Hollywood actress had just committed suicide. It so happened I was parked just three blocks from her home at the time and the proximity seemed to give the news added impact. I turned off the radio and sat in the silence of the car asking myself, "Why?" Why did she do it? Most people would think she had everything to live for. She was comparatively rich. She was exceedingly beautiful. She was famous. She had a magnificent home. She was married to a fine man, and she lived in Hollywood, U.S.A. To millions this would be just about everything they would ask from life. Yet, with all of this, life had somehow become so unendurable, such a hell on earth, that it was easier for her to die than to go on living, and she suicided!

The late Cyril S. Joad, brilliant English "Brains Truster" and philosopher, made a pertinent comment on the peril of having everything. Writing about the French Riviera where, as he puts it, "the idle rich gather like spoiled children to be amused," he says, "Like all spoiled children nothing can amuse them for long. Before an hour is over they are bored and turn to something new. They spend an hour at sunbathing, an hour at motoring, an hour at polo, an hour at cocktails, an hour at gambling. When they are bored with gambling they eat. When they are bored with eating they dance. When they are bored with dancing they make love, and when they are too bored for anything they get drunk and are put to bed. For my part," says Joad, "I do not find it surprising that the suicide rate among the unemployed rich is the highest of any class in the community."

It would seem that we need to write a large, looming question mark over much of what our generation calls "success." Yet we all pursue it so avidly. We are so busy trying to "get ahead in the world." Nobody wants to be nobody, everybody wants to be somebody. And though we would all admit in our more thoughtful moments that "you can't take it with you" and that there are some things in life more important than what is commonly called success, still we spend most of our waking hours and the best years of our lives in a quest for material gain in the hope that it may somehow bring with it that elusive thing we call happiness.

There is an almost pathetic quality about the unflagging zeal with which some people pursue a good time, mistaking it for genuine happiness. Now do not misunderstand me, I am not against fun and laughter. Heaven knows there is enough misery and heartbreak in the world without anyone draping everything with crepe and frowning upon the legitimate joys of life. But anyone who looks long at life cannot but be saddened by the throngs who, with a kind of quiet desperation, are constantly seeking happiness, a happiness that like the will-o'-the-wisp ever eludes them.

Are they not epitomized in an incident I saw at an amusement park in Toronto. It was a merry if noisy place, all ablaze with lights. The mingled roar of motors, laughter, shouts and calliopes raised a raucous hymn to twentieth-century fun. As I walked along I came upon a mother and her ten-year-old son. She was shaking him until it seemed he would fall apart and he was howling in a voice that drowned the sound around him. As I went by I caught the words, "All right, you wanted to come, and now you're going to enjoy yourself if it kills you!" Are there not thousands in our cities and on our highways who, in the desperate pursuit of happiness, are literally killing themselves "having a good time?"

Surely if happiness were the inevitable result of the acquirement of "things" Solomon would have found it. Granted that he is "the Preacher" in the book of Ecclesiastes, he had everything that life can give and had it in an abundance we can never hope to approximate. If there is happiness to be found in wealth: he sat upon a throne of solid ivory in a room plated with gold and encrusted with precious stones. If there is happiness to be found in power: he spoke, armies moved, other nations trembled. If there is happiness to be found in fame: his name was known throughout the then-known world. If there is happiness to be found in the intellectual pursuits: he had a mind we still revere to this day. If there is happiness to be found in romance: if he did not have it he should have—he certainly had enough opportunities. Here was a man with everything life can give, "pressed down, shaken together and running over," yet he looked at it and it was ashes in his hands, and he cried out, "All this is vanity and vexation of spirit."

Then there are those who try to find happiness, not so much in the things life can give, but in the experiences life may yield. This is especially a temptation to youth. It is probable that every young person has at some time in life asked the question, "Why be too concerned about religion, about moral codes and all the rest. You are only young once. Everybody sows a few wild oats. You may as well take life by the throat and seize from it every last gratification it can give. If there's something doing, count me in. If there is excitement, a new thrill, a new experience . . . I'm for it. Perhaps it does lie in the shadowland. So what? If you get away with it what difference does it make? If a lie will get you out of a jam, what's the harm? If the other fellows are bragging about their exploits with girls, why should I be a prude? If other girls get dated by lowering their moral standards, why should I sit at home alone? If you can cool a tough exam by cribbing, are you going to be a fool and go in unprepared? After all what difference does it make if you get away with it?"

But the tragic fact is that ours is a moral universe and you never do "get away" with anything contrary to the purposes of God. Sin is a strange thing; it is not finished when it has been committed. It lives on, like a termite within the soul, eating the heart out of your character and leaving you with the passage of the years a hollow sham. You do not "get away with it." The first lie breaks trail for the second and soon it becomes a well-worn path over which great falsehoods can travel. The first immorality is no bigger than a mustard seed, but it soon becomes a great, spreading growth in whose branches the grossest evils can lodge. The first dishonest act is just a ripple, but soon our lives are swamped in a tempest of deceit. This is a moral universe and "whatsoever a man soweth that shall he also reap." In the words of the old saying, "Sow a thought reap an act, sow an act reap a habit, sow a habit reap a character, sow a character reap a destiny."

It is a tragic fact that thousands of young people, trying to get the most out of life by plucking all of life's fruit— forbidden or no—are missing the best that life can give.

Then how do you get the most out of life? How do you find happiness? You turn to Jesus for light and you get a strange answer. He says, in effect, that you never find happiness by looking for it. Happiness isn't a goal, it isn't an end in itself. Happiness is a by-product of a life lived for God and others. Happiness is found, not in saving your life for yourself, but in giving it away! Listen to his words, "Whoever would save his life will lose it; and whoever loses his life for my sake . . . will save it." This is Jesus' answer to the question, "How may we get the most out of life?"—and who would know better than he?

Surely this answer sounds strange to our ears. We have gotten so wrapped up in the pressure of everyday living in this competitive world we have forgotten that life is principally a matter of direction. Life may flow either inward or outward. If it flows outward it becomes a thing of sparkling beauty and usefulness. If it flows inward in selfishness it becomes as the Dead Sea in Palestine. There is no outlet to the Dead Sea and that is why it is dead. The waters of the Jordan and the sparse rains of that locality flow into it but nothing flows out, and it is brackish and ugly. No living thing swims within its depths and no verdant foliage crowds round its edges for a drink. It is dead.

So it is with our lives when we live them only for ourselves. If all we do is done for ourselves and our own, if we are the center and circumference of our little world, our lives lose their beauty and grow increasingly frustrated and empty. It is strange, but the life that is constantly occupied in a search for its own happiness never finds it. Robert Burns put it succinctly,

> Believe me, happiness is shy,
> And comes not aye when sought, man.

The trouble is we hadn't bargained on this kind of answer. This is no gladsome invitation when Jesus bids us, "Lose your life for my sake . . . and you will find it." In our cushioned and upholstered age we shy away from hardship and inconvenience and these are uncomfortable words. We want to *find* our lives all right, but to *lose* them . . . ! That's another matter.

And yet it must be admitted that life doesn't seem to work any other way. Some time in the past we heard this call to dedicated living; perhaps in childhood, perhaps in church, perhaps in the frightening new responsibilities of parenthood or in some time of crisis, and for a while we responded. There were bright dreams back there, high resolves, noble aspirations . . . ! Remember? But then we got caught up in a swirl of responsibilities and the sounds of the very real world around us deafened our ears to the "still small voice," and we fell back. We were trying to save our life but, strangely, it has grown increasingly unrewarding and empty. And there have come moments—perhaps lying abed on a sleepless night, or at a time of disillusionment and trouble—when we have realized that what we have saved is vain and disappointing.

Can we not see our experience reflected in the life of the Apostle Peter? Jesus had called him and he had followed. But now Peter is trying to save his life in the Master's hour of greatest need. See him there in the flickering light of the campfire outside of the High Priest's Palace. A teen-age girl peers into his face and points an accusing finger. "You were with him," she cries. Jesus was losing his life in obedience

to the Father but Peter wanted to save his so, face contorted
with fear, and feigning innocence, he turns and calls down
a curse on himself. "May God strike me dead," he says in
effect, "if I ever saw that man Jesus before in my life!" He
tried to save his life but ended that night out on an abandoned
hillside weeping bitterly.

Judas tried to save his life too. It began to look as if this
whole business about a Kingdom was going to fail. After all
a fellow has to look out for himself. So, clutching the clink-
ing bag of coins, he planted that incredible kiss of betrayal
on Jesus' cheek. He tried to save his life and ended up dead
and disemboweled after hanging himself in an overpowering
surge of remorse.

There is a law here. At the heart of life there seems to be
a law that says: what you keep you lose and what you use
you have. Life is the gift of God but it is capital that must
be spent or it dissipates. That which God has given is perish-
able. It must be used. It cannot be hoarded. This is a law
of the universe. Try to keep from taxing your mind and it
grows weaker not stronger. Bind your arm to your side to
keep from wasting its strength and after a while it is shriveled
up and useless. Save up your spiritual capital and you will
soon be bankrupt. But if you use your brain it grows stronger
with the days. If you spend the strength in your arm it will
be brawny in the tomorrows. If you will lose your life in the
service of God and others you will find it in rich experience
and an ever-expanding purpose. Even as you busy yourself
living for God and, equally, for yourself and others, a deep

sense of purpose and fulfillment "sort of sneaks up on you" and suddenly you awaken to the fact that you have found life's best.

How do you get the most out of life? The answer is a simple one, a deceptively simple one: you get the most out of life by living it as it was intended to be lived . . . in a daily relationship with God. In St. Augustine's oft-quoted words, "Our lives are made for Thee, O God, and are restless until they find their rest in Thee."

Jesus, himself, is the perfect picture of selfless living and the eternal reminder that "men remember their servants and forget their kings." Is there any picture of selflessness in history comparable to that of Jesus washing the feet of the disciples. Jesus, "knowing that the Father had given all things into his hands and that he was come from God," gets down on his knees before these ignorant and illiterate disciples and washes the dirt from their travel-soiled feet! It is all the more astounding when we realize that one of those before whom he kneeled was Judas, Judas, who within the hour would hasten away on those fresh-washed feet to betray him. What a picture of humility and selfless devotion!

Look still further. Look if you will at the cross. You have looked so often, perhaps, that you no longer see it. Familiarity with the story of the crucifixion has dimmed our perception and we are not struck with horror at what we see. See him there! Does he look like the serene Jesus who has been ministering so wonderfully to the sick and the needy for the past few months? You would never recognize him did you not know it was he—"His visage marred as no other man's," his face a red smear of sweat and blood and spittle, his beard a gory tangle where they have plucked it out by the roots, his body dirty, naked and bleeding, his hands and feet pierced, his poor, tired body sagging . . . ! You would never recognize him as the One who, only a scant thirty-three years back, was a sweet-smelling babe cradled in a mother's arms. There was no hint in that cherubic face that someday it would be twisted into this ghastly mask of agony.

And now that you have taken a long look at the cross—a six-hour-long look if need be—and beyond the pain have tried to glimpse something of the spiritual agony he knew, remember this: no man took his life from him. He laid it down of himself. He deliberately, purposefully lost his life that we, in committing our life to God, might find it anew.

Whenever men look about for the perfect life, the radiant, joyful life, the truly happy life, they turn to Jesus. And yet his life led to a cross. How strange! Stranger still is the fact that those who serve only themselves, who pamper their every whim and grant license to their every appetite, are the barren and unhappy ones. Here is the great paradox: live your life selfishly and you will lose it, give it away in useful service and it grows in beauty with the years. The thirst after happiness is never quenched but in Schopenhauer's words, "there is no more mistaken path to happiness than worldliness, revelry, high life."

How may we find the best that life can give? We return to the words of Jesus, "Whoever loses his life for my sake and the gospel's will save it." Then give your life away to God and find it, full-orbed and abundant.

We are in such a great hurry, so busy about so many things we are in danger of forgetting first things. Including "everything," we leave out God. So often there is no purpose to our constant activity. Our life is a crazy quilt, made up of snippets and patches and lacking design.

❧ 8 ❧

CHROME-PLATED CHAOS

SUPPOSE by some miracle of time it were possible for you to choose the period in history in which your life would be lived—which period would you choose? Think, for instance, how thrilling it would have been to have lived back in the time of Columbus when there were yet undiscovered lands beyond the horizon. How thrilling to have lived during the American Revolution when America was coming to birth and exciting things were afoot; or in Shakespeare's time when the drama reached its height and Britain was at the zenith of her power; or in the time of Greece's glory when beauty was a commonplace and such as Plato and Aristotle would be contemporaries. I've known some young ladies who would like to have come to blossom back when knighthood was in flower, or back in the age of femininity when women were fragile and protected—and fainted at the slightest provocation. I've met many a moppet who would like to have lived when the west was wild and woolly and there was a Hopalong Cassidy on every horse.

But supposing you were to reverse things and put the question to me. When would I choose to live if I were free to choose the period in history into which I would be born?

I would choose to live . . . today! Yes, today, for despite the fact this is one of the most chaotic periods in world history it is also a day of unprecedented opportunity, a crossroads time, when, in the words of John R. Mott, "the soul of humanity is being plowed up and made ready for the planting of the seed." It is a time in which one might well cry out in despair, "Look what the world has come to!" Instead, we look to Christ and shout, *"Look what has come to the world!"*

There can be no doubt but what this is one of the crucial periods in history. The world is pivoting into a new era and is in a state of flux. Everything is new or is seen in a new perspective. We have come through a period of almost incredible scientific advance. There have been more changes in the past fifty years than in the previous two thousand years. Such have been the changes in our manner of living that a man from the last century would find our world almost unrecognizable. We live in towering skyscrapers, travel at the speed of sound, talk around the world, work on foolproof machines (one man doing the work of a hundred), amuse ourselves with such toys as cinemascope and television, and do a thousand things that H. G. Wells and Jules Verne never dreamed of in their most visionary moments.

But what has come of all this progress? How has the "brave new world" worked out? We have reacted to these blessings by having the bloodiest wars in history, by developing an unprecedented number of neuroses and psychosomatic ills, by an increasing breakdown of the marriage relationship, by a terrifying increase in juvenile delinquency, by running up the biggest liquor bill in history, by building weapons of destruction that can obliterate all civilization, and by dividing the world into two armed camps. Professor Pitirim A. Sorokin of Harvard, after a study of the more than 900 international and 1,600 civil wars of the last 25 centuries, came to the conclusion that "our own century is by far the bloodiest in history."

We are beginning to see that it is possible to make progress in *two* directions. Aldous Huxley suggests that "our technological progress allows the world to move *backward* more rapidly." If we have not actually regressed it must surely be realized that, while we have been progressing intellectually and technologically, we have fallen behind morally. We are wise but we are not good. We are full of conflicts and contradictions. We should be kings but we are the most fearful and frustrated generation in history. The age of reason has become the age of paradox.

We have knowledge but not wisdom. By "knowledge" is meant the accumulation of information. By "wisdom" is meant the correlation of that information for the good life. There can be no question but what we know more than any people in history. We have wrested from the bosom of nature ten thousand long-cherished secrets. Any modern library is a bank in which the intellectual giants of the past have made deposit and on which we may draw simply by the expenditure of a little time. Any schoolboy may learn in an hour things that the genius of another century could not learn in a lifetime. Such is the plethora of our knowledge that ours has become, of necessity, an age of specialists—no one person could begin to assimilate the available information.

But, strangely, though we have knowledge we do not have wisdom. We stand on the shoulders of the past and should be able to see the further because of it but we can't. We know all the answers but the important ones, the ones that have to do with our relationships with men and ourselves and God.

We have houses but not homes. The modern house is a far cry from the gingerbread-laden house of the Victorian era. Tremendous advances have been made and the well-designed modern home is a marvel of convenient living. Entire homes are prefabricated, gadgeted, insulated, lighted and heated in a way our fathers never dreamed of. No longer need a shivering husband tug at the clinkers, split the kindling and pamper the chimney draft to wheedle a little heat from the ash-mantled monstrosity in the basement. Once a year he touches a dial and—granted he pays his oil bill—a constant heat is maintained with no further effort. No longer does the housewife rub-a-dub-dub her laundry over a corrugated washboard at the cost of skinned knuckles and an aching back. She drops the soiled clothes into a gleaming white box, sets a dial and the laundry is automatically washed, rinsed a half-dozen times and practically hung out to dry. How did the mother of the large family of a generation ago get her work done? Before the days of electricity, steam irons and deep freezes, before automobiles, supermarkets, frozen foods, packaged goods and Sears-Roebuck, how did she get her work done? The answer is, she didn't. She was the slave of her responsibilities.

A man works from sun to sun,
But a woman's work is never done.

Things are different now. We live in compact, convenient "dwelling units," and there is time for leisure. Do we have better houses?—undoubtedly, but do we have better homes? Can we believe that we do when we study the divorce statistics? Better homes?—then why the constant lowering of the age of our criminals and an increase in juvenile delinquency that has made the streets of some American cities positively dangerous after dark? Better homes?—then why, if they are more livable, do we spend so little time in them that, in many cases, the family is not a unit?

Just as a wheel needs a hub and a planetary system a sun, so a family needs God as the center about which it congregates. A family needs a faith that unites them in love and gives them a great purpose for living. Children need a parental example. The only permanent gift a parent can give a child is the gift of character, and character is "easier caught than taught." A child is always a "chip off the old block," the pale reflection of the parents. Parents are demigods to their children and the first lessons of life are learned through the eyes and not the ears. Children will not do as we say, they will do as we do. There is no substitute for the example of a consistent Christian life.

One may be forgiven for wondering whether the modern way of raising children is an improvement. Today we bring up our children by "the book"—the most recent thought on child psychology. Let it be clear that this is no mulish, reactionary wail. None would be swifter to acknowledge the very real contribution to our understanding that has been made through the study of psychology, but "the proof of the pudding is in the eating" and it would not seem, on the basis of the evidence, that this generation of children is demonstrably superior to the generations that have preceded it—if indeed it is their equal. Lack of discipline and uninhibited freedom of expression is having its fruit in juvenile lawlessness and lack of respect for authority. There is never room for parental brutality or vengefulness but it would seem that sometimes "a good spanking" is indeed a *good* spanking. To inject a personal note: I ate many a meal from the mantelpiece for obvious physical reasons and I would doubt that it injured my personality. There were two rules in the home, the golden rule and one about so long. Both were employed regularly—a fact for which the recipient will ever be grateful.

Parental authority derives from God and our houses become homes when God is put at the center. "God hath set the solitary in families" and the home is the basic unit in a society. When a nation's homes are weak the nation is weak. "Win the family to Christian living," says Nels Ferré, "and the nation and the world is won."

We have speed but not direction. The speed with which we can travel today is an astounding thing. A generation ago a man could travel only as fast as a horse could carry him. Then came the automobile and the speed of travel increased fourfold. The airplane accelerated transportation even more and soon men were flying hundreds of miles per hour. Now a test plane is reliably reported to fly faster than 1,500 miles per hour—more than twice the speed of sound. It is now possible (theoretically) to go somewhere and hear yourself arriving; you go faster than the sound you make. You may fly from Los Angeles to New York City in a commercial airliner within eight hours. Planes cross the Atlantic in six and one half hours, a journey that took Columbus months to accomplish.

We have speed, but do we have direction? What's the hurry when we aren't sure where we are headed? In Peter Marshall's phrase, "We are saving more time than ever before but we aren't putting the time we are saving to any better use." We have better ways of going places but no better places to go, and no matter how swiftly we move we cannot get away from ourselves. We may change our location but we cannot change our nature. We take our problems along with us in sleek, silver airliners even as our forebears did in creaking covered wagons.

On the day of Pentecost the Apostle Peter stood before a crowd of thousands in Jerusalem and cried out, "Save yourselves from this untoward generation!" Any schoolboy can understand all of the words in the sentence save one. What is an "untoward" generation? Translated into simple English Peter was saying, "Save yourselves from this generation that goes round in circles, save yourselves from this meaningless whirlpool of life, from this life that is always on the go but doesn't get anywhere!" His words could be addressed to our day. We are always on the go, always in a hurry. If, a generation ago, a man missed a train he would shrug his shoulders and say, "Oh that's all right. There'll be another one along in a day or two." Today, if we go down town shopping and miss the first section of a revolving door we feel behind schedule the rest of the day. We say we are busy because our lives are full. Is it not, rather, because our lives are *empty* and we are trying to fill them up with a constant round of entertainment, excitement and sensation? Why do some women turn the radio on before breakfast and leave it on through the day? Is it not because they do not want to be alone with their thoughts, to have to take a long hard look at their home, their marriage, their children or themselves?

We are in such a great hurry, so busy about so many things we are in danger of forgetting first things. Including "everything," we leave out God. So often there is no purpose to our constant activity. Our life is a crazy quilt, made up of snippets and patches and lacking design. What's the rush when you aren't going anywhere? We tend to forget God as we forget the digit one. Who ever thinks of the digit one? And yet there is no arithmetic without it, no algebra, no geometry, no trigonometry, no calculus, no physics, no mileage, no measuring, no stocktaking, no counting, no planning, no order and no explanation. They all depend on the digit one. They have no meaning apart from the digit one. Similarly there is no meaning to the thousand things with which we fill up our life, apart from the God who created and gave meaning to that life. If in our hurry we bustle past Him we must not be surprised if suddenly life is meaningless.

We have medicines but not health. There was a time not long ago when the "prime killers" of mankind were the bacteriological diseases. The diagnosis, "Pneumonia," once sounded like a death sentence. Now, through the dedication and brilliance of men of science, these prime killers have been thrown back and are no longer the deadly threat they once were. Today men die of other causes: coronary thrombosis, cerebral hemorrhage and different kinds of organic breakdowns—in part the result of the tempo at which we live. We are beginning to see that a man is not healthy merely because he is not afflicted with an infection or incapacitated by a physical injury. There are illnesses of the mind and of the spirit.

Interestingly enough, the words "holiness" and "health" come from the same root. In the New Testament when Jesus healed a man he became "every whit whole." He was well in body, mind and spirit. Health means "wholeness" and includes the whole man. A man may be in perfect health physically and yet be mentally ill. A man may be in perfect health physically and mentally but be morally sick. Just as physical illness incapacitates a man and keeps him from doing his work so mental illness may keep him from facing up to his responsibilities and spiritual illness may keep him from finding life's best. No man is ready to meet life's challenges unless he is "every whit whole."

Men break under the pressures of living today because, in many cases, they do not have inner resources. The tempo of life in this frantic, pell-mell age crowds many beyond endurance. It is a sobering fact that one out of every two hospital beds in America is for a mental patient. There is no living without some occasional escape from pressure, without some succor in time of great trouble. When life pyramids its problems upon the Christian he falls back upon inner resources, upon the God who is able to make him to be, "strengthened with might by His Spirit in the inner man." The wind howled blusteringly at a bird as it perched singing on a twig. "I'm going to blow you off!" it shrieked. "Go ahead," sang the bird, "I have wings." So, the Christian has a source of strength beyond his own that sustains him when he gets out beyond the end of his tether.

But what of the man who does not pray? Where does he turn? Some would, of course, scorn Christianity and decry it as a "spiritual crutch" on which weaklings lean. They are epitomized by Henley's "Invictus" with its brave but tragic words,

> Out of the night that covers me,
> Black as the Pit from pole to pole,
> I thank whatever gods may be
> For my unconquerable soul.
>
> In the fell clutch of circumstance
> I have not winced or cried aloud.
> Under the bludgeonings of chance,
> My head is bloody, but unbowed.

Courageous? Yes, magnificent in its courage, but so tragically, utterly foolish. Life is often hard. It can be bitter and cruel and relentless, and the bravest soul, under the disappointments, the heartbreak, the bereavements, the failures, the anguish that life can bring will find his head not only bloody but bowed. Courageous? Yes, but foolish. Doubly foolish when a compassionate God stands ready to grant His help.

What does a man do who doesn't pray? This is what he does: he breaks under the strain and retreats from reality into mental illness, or he turns to liquor and finds a temporary escape in the illusion of well-being that alcohol brings, or he grows disillusioned and cynical; believing in nothing and hoping for nothing so he cannot be disappointed. How much they miss who do not know how to pray!

When the word came that George VI, the late King of England, was seriously ill, all of the British Commonwealth of Nations was deeply concerned. Great as that concern was it was nothing compared to what must have been felt by the Queen. To the Commonwealth the King was dying. To the Queen the King was dying—and the King was her husband, the father of her children! At that time a picture was sent out by one of the news services and printed in newspapers around the world. It was an unforgettable picture. The Queen had risen early, before dawn, and had gone to prayers at Westminster Abbey. When she came from the Abbey and got into the car to return to the Palace, one of those ubiquitous photographers stepped to the side of the car and took her picture. I have never seen an expression like the one he caught on the Queen's face. On her face there was a look of faith and tranquil peace. The King was dying, her husband was dying, but she had been to prayers and had found the inner serenity and the strength she needed in God.

I have been painting a bleak picture of our world, a world in which we have knowledge but not wisdom, houses but not homes, speed but not direction and medicines but not health. Why has our world come to this pass? Our dilemma grows out of the fact that we are lost. We have been blundering along, hoping to "muddle through," thinking that things would right themselves eventually, the while putting the blame upon the Kaiser, or Hitler, or the Communists, or the Democrats, or the Republicans, or whoever happened to be the public whipping-boy at the moment. We have gone our selfish way, looking after number one, and now we have been brought up short with the realization that we are in trouble. We are lost and there is none who knows the way out.

Abner Dean, the cartoonist-philosopher, has drawn a memorable picture of a great, yawning abyss with a number of naked people peering vainly down into the depths. One of the men is turning to say over his shoulder (to you?), "Will the three wise men please step forward?"

We are lost! And if we are ever to find the way, someone who knows the way will have to lead us out. Jesus comes and says to us as he said to others centuries ago, "I am the way."

A man was lost in the Burmese jungle. He hailed a passing native and asked the native if he would lead him out. The native said, "Follow me," and started through the jungle. Soon there was no trail and the native, swinging his machete, was hacking a path through the tangled undergrowth. Fearful, the man called ahead, "Are you sure this is the way?" The native paused a moment and then answered, "There is no way. *I* am the way. Follow me."

Jesus comes to us to say, "I am the way. Follow me." Christianity is not ten rules for living; it is Christ. He is our example, he is our teacher, he is our companion, he is our Savior . . . *he* is the way.

Do you doubt that God can transform the "average" man and make his life count? I did too until I made a study of the lives of some of the greatest men and women in history and discovered that many of them were ordinary people with ordinary talents and ordinary opportunities. There was but one extraordinary thing about them, and that was their faith in God.

❧ 9 ❧

MAKING YOUR LIFE COUNT

THE average boy is not often entranced in Sunday School.
Along with other forms of education, it is usually endured
rather than enjoyed. One boy, however, despite the passage
of many years can still remember with what avid interest he
first listened to a story related in Sunday School. It was
the exciting and unfailingly interesting story of the fight
to the finish between that ancient heavyweight champion,
Goliath of Gath, and that rising young lightweight, the
shepherd boy of Israel, David!

There they are! Goliath, a tremendous figure of a man,
head and shoulders over the rest of his people. A fierce,
mountainous, black-bearded, terrifying giant of a man, clang-
ing his spear on his shield, the lust for a fight in his eye, and, it
seems, the earth shaking beneath his feet as, armor-bearer
before him, he advances to the fray!

And there stands his slender antagonist, David! By contrast a mere stripling. Lithe and lean and bronzed by a thousand days on the hills but a mere stripling. His face is pale
beneath its tan and he looks almost comical as Saul's armor
is strapped on him. It is sizes too big and he clanks clumsily
along, looking for all the world like an animated and anemic

turtle. Then off comes the armor and clad in nothing but his shepherd's skins he moves out to meet the giant. There is no spear in his hand, no shield on his arm, no armor-bearer going before . . . nothing but a shepherd's rawhide sling swinging from one hand and five smooth stones clutched in the other.

Goliath catches his first glimpse of his opponent and throws back his head and laughs, and the laughter rolls and rumbles among the hills. "Is *this* what they send out against me?" he roars. Then the laughter slips away into a snarl and he lumbers swiftly forward. "He'll make short work of this impudent boy! He'll have done with *this* in a hurry . . . !"

There is a prayer moving softly on David's lips as, without dropping his gaze, he slips a stone into the sling. Then, suddenly, light-footed and agile as a dancer, he runs forward, whirls the sling about his head in a dizzy, whistling circle and with every ounce of strength in his wiry body sends the stone whizzing across the gap between them. It strikes the giant full between the eyes and drops him in a sprawling heap, twitching upon the ground . . . dead!

Who would have believed it? The impossible has happened! This unknown and unimpressive young shepherd boy has, singlehanded, defeated Israel's most feared enemy! An hour before you might well have asked, "What can an inconsequential youth such as this do in the face of Israel's great need?"—and now you have the answer! "What possible difference can this lad make?" you cry, and the answer comes back, *All the difference in the world!*"

This is addressed to the people who think they do not count. It is addressed to you if you sometimes tend to think of yourself as an insignificant cog in the great machinery of our civilization, as someone who can have little influence for good or bad, and if you wonder at times whether it makes any difference whether you live or die.

This is certainly a day to make a person feel insignificant. In this technological age thousands of workers are little more than an extension of a machine. You sit at a bench or a table and endlessly pack things in boxes, put tops on bottles, assemble parts, pound typewriters, file papers, wash dishes, or do any one of a thousand boring tasks.

On the way home you pick up a newspaper and you are deeply troubled by the state of the world. You have a compelling urge to *do* something but no clear idea of what can be done. The forces at work in the world seem so powerful and any one person seems so inadequate. You look and see vast empires poised to spring at one another and immense armies massed on the borders of the east and the west. You listen to the diplomats in their interminable wrangling and observe the completely different attitudes toward life and the blind refusal even to consider the other's side. And casting its shadow over the entire scene is the grim specter of The Bomb. You feel you ought to do something, you just can't stand around and let the world commit suicide . . . but what can you do?

Well, if there is nothing you can do in terms of the world situation perhaps you can do something at the heart of your own country. But then you get to thinking that you are but one among 160 million. You look at the colossus that government has become in Washington, you see the power of the major political parties, you read about the inanities of some of the legislators, you hear about corruption among officeholders and of the power of the great lobbies, and you are intimidated by it all. There is an election coming soon but it doesn't seem that one vote can make any difference so you go out of town on Election Day. After all what difference does it make?

You think perhaps you ought to pray more. But the question comes, "How do you know there *is* a God?" It certainly doesn't look like it at times. You wonder whether there is any real purpose to life or will the years just wear you out and cast you aside and let your body moulder in a forgotten grave somewhere. On days like these you wonder whether it makes any difference whether you live or die.

Of course, there is a sense in which it doesn't make much difference. You die, and the world goes on. Nobody is indispensable. Time erases the memory of all of us, whoever we are. Occasionally you get to thinking you are important and then suddenly one day you pass an abandoned cemetery and stop to look at the weeds overrunning the almost undecipherable stones, and you know that the wisest and best among us really matter to a very few.

Yes, there are a lot of things and a lot of people in life to make a person think he or she doesn't count. But if you have come to believe it, you are wrong. You *do* count, you count with God. Under God the centuries have labored to produce *you.* Jesus said that you alone are of more value than the entire world and then backed up the assertion by laying down his life for you. It matters, eternally matters, what you do with your life, how you spend your talents and your opportunities.

How can you begin to make your life count?—well, begin where you are. In the words of Jesus, "Whatsoever thy hand finds to do, *do it* with all thy might." In other words stop dreaming about great and heroic deeds and begin to do some of the thousand little tasks that lie at hand and need doing. It is a common failing to dream of doing the heroic the while neglecting the things that lie at hand. Many a young man would serve as a missionary in some far-off land but does not lift a hand to help the needy at the door. We sit around debating the giving of our whole heart and mind and strength and in the meantime fail to give even an hour of our day or a dollar of our income. We dream of touching the world and do nothing about the slum in our city. We engage in long and impassioned discussions about what the ecumenical church ought to believe and do, and do nothing to strengthen the beliefs or to extend the service of the church on the corner.

Stop dreaming of felling Goliaths and pick up some stones. Begin where you are. The way to make a journey to a distant city is to begin by taking a single step. All great achievements have humble beginnings. You begin to fly by lying on your back studying the flight of sea gulls at Kitty Hawk. You

123

begin to invent the automobile by running a bicycle repair shop in Dearborn, Michigan. You begin to discover the theory of relativity by learning the multiplication table. You begin to write *Hamlet* by learning to write. You begin to compose the Fifth Symphony by practicing your scales. Our generation is impressed by the obvious but is blind to the glory of the commonplace.

Do you doubt that God can transform the "average" man and make his life count? I did too until I made a study of the lives of some of the greatest men and women in history and discovered that many of them were ordinary people with ordinary talents and ordinary opportunities. There was but one extraordinary thing about them, and that was their faith in God.

Look, for instance, at the men who followed Jesus. Today they are honored and called "saints." What were they when Jesus called them? They were ordinary people; typical working men, fishermen, tax collectors—"common people" who heard him gladly. They were not educated. They had no money. They did not have enough influence to keep themselves out of jail. They were just "average" men, indistinguishable from the millions around them until they met Jesus. Then his faith in them called forth their faith in God and these unexciting men went out to turn the world upside down and to change the course of history!

The Bible says, "God is no respecter of persons." He is the same in every age and what He has done in the past He can do again. This is not to suggest that He will make you into a St. Peter or as one of the disciples but it is to suggest this: that if you will begin to live for Him and for His world with all your mind and heart and strength *He will do things in your life you would never have dreamed possible!* And if others will join you in the same resolve He can once again change the course of history.

"But," you say, "I am so insignificant." So was David. So is an atom. Yet there is enough latent power in the atoms of a thimbleful of water to drive an ocean liner to Europe and back.

"But," you say, "I am so unstable and weak." So was David. So is water. Yet let some water trickle into the crack of a rock and freeze and it will split the largest boulder on a mountainside.

"But," you say, "I am so inconsequential." So was David. So is a snowflake, a fragile little flower crystal, so light as to hardly move the most delicate scale. Yet it is one flake of snow joined with dozens and millions of others that blocks highways, halts the mightiest locomotives, cuts off the greatest cities and blankets a continent with white. Unimportant as your life may seem, impossible as the challenge may appear, unequipped as you may seem to be, the promise is, "With God all things are possible!" He is able to give us the wisdom to know what can be done and the strength to do it.

Let me give you an example of how God uses "the weak things of the world to confound . . . the mighty." Come with me to the city of Boston back before the turn of the century. We enter a shoe store and stand behind a display so that we may see but not be seen by one of the clerks at the back of the store. He is certainly not a prepossessing man. There is nothing impressive about him except his size; he weighs more than two hundred pounds. He is anything but handsome. He has a thick black beard that falls to his chest. His eyes are too closely set together. His nose is broad, his features are coarse. When he speaks it is like a machine gun; two hundred words a minute. His speech is full of grammatical errors. Until the day he dies he will say, "He don't" instead of "He doesn't," "He ain't" instead of "He isn't." There are in existence letters he wrote during the last years of his life in which he misspells the commonest English words. There is good reason for it, he never finished the eighth grade in school.

Now let me tell you something of this young man. One of these days this uneducated, unprepossessing young man, without any further training, is going to go on a tour of the United States and Great Britain. He is going to make speeches. Every time he rises to his feet ten to twenty thousand people will flock to hear him. Kings and presidents and prime-ministers will sit at his feet. He will speak in the highest institutions of learning in the world. And when his life is finished it will be estimated that the lives of at least a million people have been changed because he passed by.

"Impossible!" you say, "Impossible! If this illiterate, eighteen-dollar-a-week shoe clerk could do this it would be little short of a miracle!" Exactly! But the miracle happened, and you will understand when I tell you the shoe clerk's name.

He is Dwight L. Moody, the greatest evangelist since the Apostle Paul and a man of unparalleled Christian dedication.

How did it happen? It happened because this young man decided he must help others to find God. He sat on a platform, almost unknown, while an Englishman by the name of Henry Varley was preaching. Varley said, "The world yet waits to see what God can do with a man who will dedicate his entire life to Him." Behind him on the platform Moody bent his great head and prayed, "God, I will be that man." Then he began where he was. He sought permission to teach a Sunday school class of boys. There was no class without a teacher and he was denied. So he cleaned up a space in the basement of the church, went out and gathered the roughest boys from the streets round about and formed his own class. There was no waiting for the world to come to him, no daydreaming about the exciting things that might be done, no bemoaning the lack of opportunity. The beginning was a circle of ragged street boys gathered in the dark corner of a furnace room. But the circle expanded until it encompassed millions. "Whatsoever thy hand finds to do . . . *do it!*"

Is it ridiculous to hold out the hope that one person can do something to meet the great needs of our time? In our great impersonal world can we really believe in the influence of the individual? Well, apparently we believe in the influence of the individual *communist*. America is spending millions of dollars to root individual communists out of government. We seem convinced that one man, if he is a Communist, can affect the destiny of a nation as great and powerful as the

United States. If we believe that one person can influence the nation for wrong why do we doubt that one person can influence the nation for right? Is there more vitality in the faith of the communist than in the faith of the Christian?

It is time we ceased to study the difficulties and began to envision the opportunities. When the Israelites came to the borders of the Promised Land they sent out an advance party to determine what dangers lay ahead. They returned with two widely disparate reports. The majority report was discouraging. "There are giants in the land," they cried, "and we are as grasshoppers in their sight!" Caleb brought a minority report. "There *are* giants in the land," he said, realistically, "and their cities are walled and very great, but we are well able to overcome it." The difference was a matter of perspective. The majority saw the problem in terms of their own weakness; "There are giants in the land and we are *in their sight* as grasshoppers." Caleb saw the difficulties in terms of God's strength; "There are giants in the land and they are *in God's sight* as grasshoppers."

We get a different view of life when God is in the picture and when we realize that the ultimate worth of a thing does not lie in its intrinsic value but in its usefulness. Bread actually is more valuable than diamonds. Water is more precious than rubies. Farmers are more important than movie stars. You would not think so to read the headlines but we know it is so. Even so, our apparently lacklustre lives have a value that often escapes us. Our lives are God's opportunity. Insignificant as we may seem, we are the instruments God has fashioned to use in the achieving of His will on earth. And it is not the instrument that matters; it is the skill and power of the one who uses it.

A great violinist stood before an audience and enraptured them with his playing. Suddenly, in the midst of the selection, he paused, took the violin from beneath his chin, raised it in the air, and smashed it into a thousand pieces upon the floor. The audience sat aghast. In the silence the violinist walked to the front of the platform and said quietly, "Don't be alarmed. The violin I smashed was one I purchased for a few dollars in a department store. I shall now play upon the Stradivarius." He took the valuable instrument from the case, tuned it for a moment and began to play. The music was magnificent, but to the majority of those present it was indistinguishable from the earlier selection. When he had concluded, the violinist spoke again. "Friends," he said, "so much has been said about the value of this violin in my hands that I wanted to impress upon you the fact that the music is not in the instrument, *it is in the one who plays upon it*."

So it is with us. In the final analysis it is not our great gifts that matter—some with great gifts are using them improperly—it is what God is able to do with us. You see a sunset and you say, "How beautiful!" But do you know what makes a sunset? It is the dust and the tiny drops of vapor in the air; these commonplace things make the glory of a summer sunset. Not the dust and vapor alone, not the sun alone, but these commonplace things transformed by the magnificence of the sun.

Longfellow could take a worthless sheet of paper and write a poem on it and make it worth thousands of dollars. That is genius. John D. Rockefeller could take a worthless check and write his name on it and make it worth millions. That is wealth. A craftsman can take material worth but a few cents and fashion an article worth a thousand times as much. That is skill. An artist can take a fifty-cent piece of canvas and a dollar's worth of pigment and paint a picture worth a fortune. That is art. God can take an ordinary life, change it and make it a blessing to the entire world. That is the grace of God!

David's greatness did not lie in David alone. David was but a penniless shepherd boy. It was not David alone, but David plus God. God provides the ability and the opportunity and the rest is up to us.

There is a fable about a very wise man who lived on the outskirts of a little town in a humble shack. Such was his wisdom that people came from all over the world to ask him questions. Always he gave them the right answer. There was a boy who lived in the town. He did not like the wise man—nobody likes anybody who is right all the time—and he decided he would ask a question the wise man could not answer. He would snare a bird and, holding it alive in his hand, would say, "Mr. Wise Man, is this bird alive or is it dead?" If the wise man said it was dead, he would open his hand and let the bird fly away. If the wise man said it was alive, he would give his hand a quick squeeze and open it to show the bird dead. No matter what the wise man said, he had him.

So he snared a bird and, holding it in his hand, said to the wise man in that guileless way that only a boy can feign, "Mr. Wise Man, is this bird dead or is it alive?" Strangely, the wise man did not look at his hand. Instead, he looked full into the boy's eyes and said quietly, "My son . . . it's whatever *you* want it to be."

So it is with us. "The world yet waits to see what God can do with a man who will dedicate his entire life to Him."

The hope of stumbling upon a ready-made happiness disregards a principle at the heart of life: life is not what you find, it is what you create. We are born with two things, existence and opportunity, and these are the raw materials out of which, under God, we can make a worth-while life.

10

TRADING PEARLS FOR PEBBLES

EVERYONE loves a good story. Take any child on your knee and invent a story; if you are even passably good at it, when you come to the words, "and so they lived happily ever after," the child will invariably look up into your face and say, "Tell me another one."

However, this enjoyment of a good story has nothing to do with age. People of all ages, of every generation, of every nation in history have listened to and been regaled by a good story. Jesus knew this. Consequently, when he wanted to teach he used stories. In the Bible these stories are called parables and while a parable is more than a story, that is essentially just what it is—a good story that catches at the sleeve of your imagination and makes concrete and clear things otherwise difficult to understand.

Centuries ago Jesus told a story about a fabulous pearl. The entire story, as it is recorded in the Bible, is but one sentence long: "The kingdom of heaven is like a merchant in search of fine pearls, who, on finding one pearl of great value, went and sold all that he had and bought it."

As Jesus spoke there must have arisen in the imagination of his hearers a picture of an Oriental bazaar. The bazaar, or market place, of the Orient is a fascinating place and remains today just what it was in Jesus day: a seething scene of men, women, children and animals crowded together into an ancient market place—the picture indescribable, the tumult of sound unbelievable and the smell unbearable!

The nearest equivalent in America is the small-town Saturday of years ago. Dressed in your Sunday best you hitched up the mare or got the Model T to percolating and drove into town—ostensibly to shop, but that was just the obvious reason—and parked alongside the board sidewalk on Main Street, where you passed the time of day, caught up on the local news and watched the passing parade. Take a small-town Saturday, change the stores into flapping tents, the cars into oxcarts, the horses into camels; fill the air with a thousand sounds and sights and smells, and there you have it . . . an Oriental bazaar!

Of course buying and selling at the bazaar was very different than in our world of commerce. It was not at all like one of our modern supermarkets, where you fill up a wire go-cart with a selection of uniform goods and push the load to a slotted counter where a bored young lady in dispassionate indifference tots up the total on a mechanical marvel and shoves a slip of paper at you on which the price is plainly marked, and that is that.

It was not like that at the bazaar. There were no fixed prices. If you saw something you wanted you inquired as to the price. The merchant would name a price twice what he expected to get and you would make an offer of half what you intended to pay. Then began the bargaining; a prolonged process that might extend over half a day, accompanied by much gesticulation, constant appeals to heaven to witness the perversity of the thief with whom you have been thrown and insults to the ancestors of this robber who would so grievously cheat you. Then, finally, agreement was reached. You paid what you expected to and the merchant pocketed what he hoped to get and everybody was happy. It was not only the way of doing business in those days but it was the entertainment of that time as well.

Into a scene like this comes the pearl merchant of Jesus' story. The moment he makes an appearance the word moves swiftly from flapping booth to flapping booth along the crowded way, "The jeweler is here!" He was an exotic man who traveled the then-known world buying and selling precious stones. If you caught him in the right mood he could recount fascinating tales of distant places.

Now as he moves among the crowd his robes flap about his cadaverous body. His face is lean and lined and bronzed by constant exposure to the oriental sun. His dark, beady eyes dart swiftly from booth to booth, his practiced gaze missing nothing. Then suddenly he sees it! His entire body stiffens almost imperceptibly. A pearl! But such a pearl!—lustrous, large, beautifully formed, perfect. And suddenly he knows, "This is it!—the dream pearl, the flawless jewel for which he has searched a lifetime!" With studied casualness he walks over to the booth, inquires about the price of other stones and then casually, almost indifferently, he picks up the pearl, hefts it in his palm and asks the price. The merchant names a price. With no change of expression to betray the seething excitement within, he makes a swift mental calculation and realizes . . . it will cost him everything he has.

Then the haggling begins. He spills out a little heap of amethysts, adds some garnets and a few rubies. What of these in exchange for the pearl? The merchant scorns him. He adds more stones, some coins, and the merchant calls on heaven to witness the insult. A half-dozen times he feigns to walk away only to be drawn back when the merchant calls after him. He must have the pearl! Finally, after much doubting and debating with himself, he turns out his pockets, spills all of his gems onto the counter and the deal is closed. The pearl is his! It has cost him everything he has but now he owns "the pearl of great price"!

There are many interesting facets to this ancient story. Among other things is not Jesus suggesting that life is a market place in which you may get what you want so long as you are ready to pay for it? Every day in the market place of life we are spending something of infinite value. Do we not speak of "spending" time? A man "spends" his life in a particular quest. We "spend" our energies, our abilities and our strength in the pursuit of our goals. Life is our capital and we spend it every day. The question is, What are you getting in exchange for your life? What are the things you count so valuable you are willing to spend your entire life to get them?

One would fear that a great many people are being taken

in. They are getting pebbles rather than pearls. There are millions who will buy anything just so long as it is new, modern, up to date, the last word. They have a disdain for anything old, anything that is not wrapped in cellophane and fresh from the assembly line. If they own a car it must be this year's model. If they read a book it must be on the best-seller list. Their clothes must be in the current *Vogue* or *Esquire*. The latest movie is the best one. The most recent editorial opinion is the truth. Fallen prey to the advertising copywriter and entranced by the scientific gadgetry of their day they act as though wisdom was born this morning and anything older than yesterday is outmoded.

Americans have a unique penchant for new things. We like to be abreast of the times. This tendency has been shrewdly exploited in a sign by a Maine roadside that reads, "BE UP TO DATE! GET YOUR ANTIQUES AT SAWYERS!" This desire for contemporaneity is, of course, a legitimate thing, so long as it is balanced by the knowledge that written over history are the words, "Everything changes! Nothing changes!" The fundamentals of life do not change though the trappings and the scenery may. The man of today may drive a Cadillac instead of a chariot, he may wear a suit from Brooks Brothers instead of a toga by Omar the Tentmaker but beneath the external differences he is the same man, with the same drives, the same problems and the same needs. And the answers to life which Jesus propounded to his contemporaries are still valid despite the passage of two thousand years. The years have brought many new insights and an augmented understanding but the fact yet remains that life apart from God is barren and pointless. Our generation, that so blithely cast aside the Christian answers as archaic, would be well advised to dust off its Bible and, retaining all of our recent insights, bring itself up to date on the ultimate answers to life.

There are other things for which we spend our lives. A great many among us seek financial security. It may well be that the unique sin of our time is the sin of avarice. Millions spend their time and their energies in an attempt to get rather than to give. In the market place of life they trade their life for dollars.

Who can reckon what dark deeds have been done for a dollar or an accumulation of dollars! The crimes that have been committed, the virtue that has been stolen, the laws that have been corrupted, the lives that have been warped in the pursuit of the Almighty Dollar! Little wonder Jesus had more to say about possession than about Heaven. It is so easy to forget that while making a living you are also making a life.

This is no silly tirade against money as such. The New Testament does not condemn money; it is the *love* of money, the inordinate concern for money, that receives the opprobrium, "the root of all evil." To those who say flippantly, "After all, what's money?" the answer is, money is a magnificent boon. It is peace of mind for the impoverished. It is help for the helpless. It is food for the hungry. It is an Aladdin's Lamp by which we may achieve a thousand wonders.

Money is a magnificent servant, but it is a dangerous master, and if we are not careful the shine of it will blind our eyes to other things and the clink of it will deafen our ears to other sounds.

Our generation seems especially subject to the illusion that money can provide security. The deep-seated uncertainty of the atomic age has produced an abnormal interest in security. Possibly the most disquieting fact revealed in any poll of recent years is that first on the list of things wanted by teen-agers today is security! How incredible that young people on the threshold of life should be most concerned to seek, not challenge, but security!

One would not belittle the desire for financial security or suggest that we ought not to prepare for the future. The Apostle Paul states that he who fails to provide for his family's future is "worse than an infidel." When Jesus said, "Take no thought for the morrow," he did not mean that we ought not to be provident, but rather that we must not worry about tomorrow's troubles today. It is proper to plan for the future but it is an illusion to believe that any amount of money or any accumulation of possessions can provide security. When you come to the real problems of life there is no buying security.

A wealthy businessman whose son was seriously ill came to his physician terribly distraught. "Doctor," he said, "save my boy. Spare no expense. If you have to fly in the most brilliant men in the field, do so. If you have to get special equipment, order it. I don't care what it costs, save my boy's life!" The doctor took him by the hands and quieted him. "There isn't a thing in the world you can buy him, except one dollar and sixty cents worth of medicine," he said quietly, "and anyone can buy that. Everything humanly possible has been done for your boy. There is nothing to do now but wait. Your boy's life is in the hands of the God who gave it to him. Slip off by yourself somewhere and talk to your Heavenly Father about your son. Incredible as it may seem, He loves your boy more than you do. Put your son's life in the hands of Him who gave it and trust Him."

I have a friend in Toronto with whom I attended high school and then art school. He left school to become a sign painter. Later he got into the used-car business. It was during the period just prior to the war when cars were scarce and expensive. Within a few years he was comparatively wealthy. He bought a boat, a luxurious cruiser, with which to travel the Canadian lakes. On the maiden journey, with his family aboard, he touched the starter. There was a short circuit, a blinding explosion and the boat was enveloped in a boiling blanket of flame. He managed to push his wife and one of his sons overboard to safety but his other son was burned to death. Months later we were playing golf together. Standing on the tee waiting for the foursome in front of us to get out of range, he told me the story of the fire and recounted how a well-meaning friend, trying to cheer him up, had said, "Well, Ted, there's one thing to be grateful for. Your boat was insured. You didn't lose your money." I shall never forget his expression as he relived the moment. The blood had drained from his face and his skin was gray. Tears ran down his checks unnoticed and his voice broke. "What did I care about my money," he said, "about *all* of my money! My boy was . . . gone!"

You cannot buy security. Of what use is money when you come to the great crises of life; when the doctor looks you full in the eyes and says gently, "I'm sorry but you have cancer"; when the telephone rings and an obviously disguised voice says, "Maybe this is none of my business but I think you ought to know your husband is not faithful to you"; or when there is a policeman at the door saying, "You'd better come down to the station, your son is in serious trouble." When you are staggering under the terrible blows that life can deal, of what use is money?

It is a simple fact that there is no security in an atomic age. Where can security be found in an atomic age?—nowhere but in God. At a time when, in Albert Einstein's words, "there exists the distinct possibility of the contamination of the atmosphere by radioactivity to where life on this planet would cease to exist," in a generation where there is "nowhere to hide," the only possible security lies in the realm of Christian character. It consists in the knowledge that your life is in God's hands, in the assurance that the Creator and Sustainer of all life is your Heavenly Father, and that despite every external evidence to the contrary He stands behind the scenes guiding the destiny of the nations. Here alone is security found in an atomic age.

Moreover, is Jesus not implying in his story that the pearl

merchant had a purpose. He counted one thing of supreme value and he let nothing stand in the way of his achieving it.

Most of us live otherwise. Millions live with no central purpose in life. We go through life, one day following uneventfully on the heels of the day before, in the hope that, someday, we will stumble onto a ready-made happiness. Life will be good, someday, "when our ship comes in." If only I could make more money, if only I lived in a decent house, if only I could get that job, if only I could travel, if only I could get married . . . if only I could get my divorce!—everything would be different.

The hope of stumbling upon a ready-made happiness disregards a principle at the heart of life: Life is not what you find, it is what you create. We are born with two things, existence and opportunity, and these are the raw materials out of which, under God, we can make a worth-while life. You never *find* happiness, just as you never *find* steel; you fashion it out of the rough ore. You never *find* a beautiful statue; you carve it out of the rough marble. You never *find* great music; you compose it out of the eight-note scale. Existence and opportunity are the raw materials out of which, under God, you can make a worth-while life. You get a mind; you can use it or let it stagnate. You get 365 days in the year; you can waste them or use them. You get two people living together in that incredible proximity we call marriage; you can turn it into a beautiful relationship or you can make it a hell on earth. You get a great Savior; you can put him at the heart of life or crowd him out to the edges. You do not find happiness, you create it.

Millions let life slip through their fingers because they have no purpose. Their life is like a boxful of scattered beads with no thread to hold them together. They are like the little girl who was given five dollars with which to buy herself a present. All afternoon she wandered through a department store, seeing so many things she wanted but never quite able to make up her mind. When the end of the day came, she found herself locked out of the store, her face pressed wistfully against the glass of the door. Her money was still in her purse and she had not bought a thing.

There are a great many who go through life the same way, seeing so many things they want, always intending to do something about it but never getting it done. Then one day they come to the twilight slope of life and suddenly realize with stunning impact that they have wasted their life. Their intentions were good. They expected someday to read that book, to cultivate that taste for good music, to break off that wrong relationship, to have done with that bad habit, to dedicate themselves to God, but it never seemed to get done. Then suddenly they are in the twilight of life and face to face with the fact that life is gone. All those years and nothing of consequence to show for it.

It was not so with the pearl merchant. He knew what was to him supremely valuable. He spent his life in a search for it and when he found it he let nothing stand in the way. Jesus tells us that the "pearl of great price" is the Kingdom of God—

the presence of God's spirit within our lives. If God is with us life has meaning and purpose. If He is absent life is empty no matter how rich its trappings or how filled with honors its hours. Have we found this pearl, without which all of life's jewels are pebbles and with which each new day is a new-strung gem in a necklace of ever-increasing beauty?

The story is told of an American millionaire who was exceedingly anxious to break into high society. Despite his great wealth he was constantly rebuffed. He decided to travel to Europe to add to his culture. On the return journey aboard a great ocean liner he would, during his morning promenade, try to break into a close-knit group of society people customarily on deck at the hour. Each day they would snub him afresh. One morning he broke into their circle and, just as they were turning away, spilled out onto his palm from a small chamois bag, a pearl. The entire group turned. Such a pearl! They had never seen such a pearl. Where had he purchased it? He was the center of all eyes. He told the story of the pearl; a story filled with history and intrigue. The pearl had once been set in a famous crown and now it had come to him. Recounting the story, he absent-mindedly hefted the pearl in his hand. There was a gasp. Was he not afraid it might fall to the deck and roll over the side? In disdain he tossed the pearl even higher. Suddenly it dawned upon him that every eye was fixed on him. The gaze of these people he so much wanted to impress was focused upon him, and there was astonishment in their eyes. He threw the pearl even higher. It looped up into the light and down again. He caught it. They were watching him, simply transfixed. Carried away, he threw the pearl still higher. Up it sped, seemed to hesitate, and then sped downward to his hand. He had it. He stretched out his hand to catch it. As he did the ship lurched and the pearl sped through his outstretched fingers, bounced high in the air, looped over the rail and down into the dark waters, gone forever. And he stood there like the fool he was . . .

Do we not stand in the same danger: the pearl of great price within our reach, the offer of God's presence awaiting our response and, enraptured with other things, we let life's greatest gift slip through our fingers? "The kingdom of heaven is like a merchant in search of fine pearls, who, on finding one pearl of great value, went and sold all that he had and bought it."

There for our encouragement stands "the disciple whom Jesus loved." John is not a miracle, he is a man: but a man plus God! And any one of us can be that.

11

SAINT WITH MUSCLES

I HAVE a grudge against artists. That may seem strange in the light of the fact that I spent five years of my life as a commercial artist and would normally be well disposed to men and women so facile with brush and pencil. The grudge grows out of the disservice artists have rendered the Church.

It is admitted, of course, that we stand forever in their debt, for they have beautified our sanctuaries, enhanced our worship and ennobled our concepts in a thousand ways. But they have helped to bring a note of unreality to the entire message of the Christian Church by portraying the events of Bible times as though the entire story is something from the "never-never-land" of fairy tales. There are already more than enough organizations in the world but, facetiously, we might well found another. It would be called "The Society to Banish Halos from Religious Pictures." If it does its work well perhaps a great many people will begin to see that the story of Jesus and the Christian Church is not something removed from everyday life but is as down to earth and practical as potatoes.

A case in point is the man with whom we are concerned here. He is a fascinating and tremendously vital personality, but because he has frequently been portrayed as an effeminate dreamer the inspiration of his life has often been lost.

In all likelihood the trouble arises out of a phrase applied to him during his lifetime. He was known among his circle of acquaintances as "the disciple whom Jesus loved." Could anything finer be said of a man? But our difficulty lies in the fact that these are familiar words and because of their familiarity the full implication does not immediately break on us. "The disciple whom Jesus loved" . . . But Jesus loved *everyone*, didn't he? Of course he did. Everyone! It did not matter if they were diseased, adulterous, criminal, or poverty stricken; he loved them all. Of course he loved some with a special love: Lazarus, at whose grave he wept, children, to whose defense he always came, his mother, whom he remembered in the utter agony of his last hours on the cross. This, then, is the amazing thing about John: if Jesus loved these others so much, how he must have loved John if he could be identified by simply referring to him as "the disciple whom Jesus loved"!

He is an intriguing man when you come to know him. Let us attempt to bring him to life upon these pages that we may draw from his life the inspiration that is there.

First, get a mental picture of the man. No one has been more inadequately portrayed. In Leonardo da Vinci's masterpiece, "The Last Supper," while it would seem the artist has perfectly portrayed both Judas and Peter, John is pictured as a meek, unassuming weakling. Nothing could be further from the truth!

The artist's misconception probably grows out of two or

three events in scripture which have been magnified out of
proper importance. First, the fact that at the Last Supper he
is reported as "leaning on Jesus' breast." Second, as has been
noted, he is referred to as "the disciple whom Jesus loved."
Third, the fact that the New Testament books which bear
his name are filled with the word "love" and have about them
a more mystical quality than all the others. But do not be
misled. Let no one turn aside from this tremendous figure of
a man because he has sometimes been portrayed as effeminate
and weak. He is no weakling, no sissy. You may be absolutely
certain about that.

You can catch a hint of that fact in the nickname Jesus gave
him. Jesus frequently renamed his disciples when they joined
his little band. What did he call John? He called him "Son
of Thunder."

You can see the reason for the name in three events in
John's association with Jesus. Scene one. John comes bustling
up to the Master. The disciples had come upon a man who
was traveling about performing cures and claiming the
authority of Jesus to do it. John reports officiously and in no
uncertain terms, "We forbade him, for he does not follow
us!" Scene two. Jesus, followed by a great crowd, is on his
way to Jerusalem. They must pass through the little country
of Samaria. John and others are sent ahead to arrange accom-
modations for the night. The Samaritans refuse to allow them
to stop in town. So back comes this "Son of Thunder," his face
lowering, lightning flashing from his eye. There must be
retaliation. "Let us call down fire from heaven and destroy

them!" is his gentle suggestion. Scene three. John and his brother James—ambitious and strong willed—arrange, through their mother Salome, an interview with Jesus. What do they want, some little favor, some trivial boon? Nothing of the kind. They want to arrange to sit on the chief seats in the coming Kingdom. Vice-presidents is what they want to be! Nothing less! Jesus responds by asking them whether they are ready to share also the agony that lies ahead, and in brash self-assurance they answer, "We are!"

As you can see, this man is no sentimental dreamer, no aesthetic, soft-eyed sissy. John is a strong-willed, hot-tempered, positive personality.

Other than this what does the New Testament record reveal about this man and his background. The first thing you notice as you study him is his reticence concerning himself. Though he played a leading part in the drama his writings never refer to him by name. Moreover, he never mentions his brother's name, nor his mother's.

Despite this reserve we know a number of facts about him. His father's name was Zebedee, his mother's Salome. His mother was a sister to the Virgin Mary and this would make John a cousin to Jesus. It would also relate him to John the Baptist through Elisabeth. This makes it easy to understand Jesus' words on the cross when he told John to look after his mother; Mary was John's aunt and it is thus quite normal that he would take her to his home after the crucifixion.

There are other known facts about John. He was a fisherman. With his brother James and his father Zebedee he was in the fishing business. Their partners were Andrew and Peter who also became disciples. There is every reason to believe that John was reasonably prosperous. His father could afford hired servants. His mother is referred to as "a woman of means"—one of a number of such who ministered to Jesus' necessities. He had a home in Jerusalem in which he sheltered Peter after his denial and to which, in all likelihood, he took Mary when she was committed to him at the cross. There is yet another hint that he was a successful man; it is clear that he was "a friend of the High Priest." As a matter of fact, it was John who spoke to the maiden at the door of the palace and had Peter let into the enclosure during Jesus' trial.

So here is our picture of the man: a relatively successful businessman with calloused hands who moved among people of importance. A dominant, affectionate, aggressive man, but with something of the mystic about him. Moreover, as we shall see, he is a man of great courage and deep loyalty. Quite a man! Little wonder millions have been intrigued by him across the centuries.

But now we ask ourselves, why was John especially beloved by Jesus? Was it not, first of all, because of his faith? In all likelihood he had known his cousin Jesus through childhood, had seen him grow, had played with him in his teens, but from the day he heard John the Baptist cry, "Behold the Lamb of God," he began to follow Jesus as Lord and, so far as we know, he never doubted or forgot. And that took faith!

Do you think it was easy for John to believe? Would it be

easy for you to believe that your cousin is divine? How often John's racing mind must have said, "But he's my cousin! I know his mother; she's my own Aunt Mary! Why, I've watched him grow. I've seen him studying. I know the little carpenter's shop in which he used to work. I remember the day he cut his hand on a chisel . . . !" Was it easy for John to believe? It was more difficult than it is for you or me. But he *did* believe, and his faith never appeared to falter.

It would seem that Jesus holds a special love for those who have faith in him. He loves all mankind, it is true, but he has a special love for those who love him. If you would know the wonder of being beloved of God have faith in His Son. Trust your life to him in an act of faith. Begin to live according to his will in home, in school, in business, in every area of life. If you believe him to be the Son of God then serve him. Don't just sing hymns to him or say little prayers—important as this may be—but live for him. And if you will, you will come to know something of the special love he expresses to those who love and serve him.

Moreover, was not John especially beloved because of his courage and loyalty? It has been often said that all of Jesus' disciples forsook him and fled in his hour of greatest trial. There is some truth to it. You can lay something to the charge of all of them—Peter, Thomas, Judas . . . every one.

But the charge is not entirely true. John may have quailed for a moment when the soldiers came to arrest Jesus in the Garden, for the record says, "They all forsook him and fled." But it must be remembered that his courage came swiftly flooding back and with the heart of a lion he followed Jesus into the courtyard and right to the foot of the cross. The Gospel reads, "Jesus therefore . . . saw the disciple standing by, whom he loved."

We have seen that he was an affectionate man, a direct, straightforward man, and now we see him to be a man of courage. Can you imagine what comfort it must have brought to Jesus, his eyes covered with a film of pain, to look down and see, amid the sea of faces filled with hatred and scorn, the compassionate face of John.

Did it take courage to stand there? You can measure how much by the fact that the others ran away. And does it take courage to stand with Christ today? Ah yes it does! It takes a peculiar brand of moral courage which, without ostentation, seeks to understand and to do the will of God each day. It takes that strong but gentle courage which, without feigning an unnatural piety, brings God into every relationship in life. It is that courage with humility that stands for justice and decency and human rights even if it means standing against the prevailing opinion. It is that uniquely Christian courage that continues to work for good even if there is little evidence that it is nearing accomplishment.

Does it take courage to be truly Christian? You can measure how much by the numbers on the rolls of the Church who draw back from the dedication it demands. Christianity is not—as many believe—an escapist faith especially suited for parsons, the aged and the very young. It takes the finest kind of manhood and womanhood truly to follow Christ. If anyone thinks it is easy let him try it. Let him seriously try to bring the principles and attitudes of Jesus to his daily life for a day, a week, a month. It takes courage; the highest kind of courage. But God loves the courageous, the Church needs the courageous, and the world is changed by the courageous!

But perhaps the principal reason for Jesus' unusual love of John was the apostle's gentleness. He was a strong and rugged man and yet there was a strain of tenderness in his make-up. This may be the reason he best interprets the love of God. If you want to understand the theology of the Gospel, read Paul. If you want to understand the importance of ethics and deeds, read James. But if you want to know something of the self-giving love of God . . . to whom else can you go but to John!

But it is no sentimental gush when John speaks of God's love. John is a sensitive man but he is no sentimentalist. He knows God's love is boundless but he knows also that it is demanding and often stern. And this is something we have forgotten. In recent decades men have done a great deal of wishful thinking about God. God is good—that we know—and we have gone on from this to suggest that, because He is good, He is too good to judge us. But we must see, not only the goodness but the severity of God. God's overtopping attribute is love. We overlook, however, the fact that it is this same love that makes Him inflexible in His opposition to wrong. We tend to sentimentalize the love of God, to make it a soft and flaccid thing. The God of many persons these days is all gushing sentimentality, sweetness and light; not a Father in Heaven but, as someone has suggested, "a Grandfather in Heaven," overlooking our wilfulness and planting a kiss of pardon on our infuriated little brow even as we resist His will. This is all very lovely but it is also very shallow and very incorrect.

It does not take a very penetrating insight to see the judgment of God in history. Even the most cursory look will reveal that the universe is designed to operate in a certain way within the eternal purposes of God. You keep the physical "laws" or you get hurt. You keep the law of love in your human relationships or you get hatred and conflict. You live life under God's lordship or your life becomes increasingly confused and empty. The judgment of God is no vindictive ecclesiastical bogey designed to win conformity; it is fundamental to life. John knew this. He saw the love of God in the life and death of Jesus but he also saw the judgment of God there and he never preached the one without the other. Our difficulty is that we have never taken sin seriously and have talked ourselves into believing that God does not either.

But what was the result of this special love that Jesus had for John? Did it mean a release from trouble and pain and struggle? It meant nothing like that. Christianity does not remove you from the world and its problems; it makes you fit to live in it, triumphantly and usefully. The Christian is not absolved from suffering; who has known such suffering as Jesus himself—"Man of Sorrows" that he was. Nor does it promise perfect human relationships; Jesus was "hated and despised among men" who were not satisfied until they had nailed his flesh to a cross.

It is clear that John did not escape life's trials. It is true that he outlived all of the other disciples and, so far as we know, was the only one of the Twelve who was not martyred, but he spent his last years in exile and for a man of John's temperament, with the great love of others that burned within him, would that not be harder to endure than sudden death? Can you not imagine him sitting by the shore on the Isle of Patmos watching the waves break upon the rocks, and each wave reminding him of the waves on the Sea of Galilee and each silvered pool seeming to mirror the faces of all those from whom he was separated by the miles. Perhaps that is why, as has been suggested, when he wrote of Heaven he said. "There shall be no more sea."

How terrible for a man like John to be alone! Life for the disciple Jesus loved was not easy, but it was triumphant. For in his loneliness there came a vision, a vision that swung open the door into the world beyond and hinted at the afterlife. And who would not welcome the hardships when they are followed by an Apocalypse!

So it is with us. Who would forego the mountaintop experiences of life just to be rid of the valleys? Who would escape to Heaven on "a flowery bed of ease" when there are challenges to be met and tasks to be done? As with John, life is not easy but it can be triumphant. The Christian does not live in a different world but makes a different world out of the one he lives in. And there for our encouragement stands "the disciple whom Jesus loved." John is not a miracle, he is a man: but a man plus God! And any one of us can be that.

It seems to me we have heard more than enough sermons on man's depravity. In other days the preacher labored to do one thing: to convince the hearer that he was a sinner. I want you to see the other side of the picture, I want you to see that God believes in you. He knows you better than you know yourself and He believes in you.

❦ 12 ❦

GOD BELIEVES IN YOU

THERE can be no doubt about it, some of the people who live within the pages of the Bible just don't seem to belong in church. You open the pages and a motley assortment shuffles forth: harlots, lepers, beggars, cripples, corrupt politicians, thieves . . . Look at them!—a straggling band of despised misfits, some the very dregs of the society of which they were a part, the community flotsam and jetsam of their day. Somehow they don't seem to belong in church.

And yet, strangely, many of them were friends of Jesus. He seemed perfectly at home with them. Nothing seems more natural than Jesus in the presence of the morally and physically diseased. The perfect frame for a portrait of the Master is a circle of what the Bible calls "sinners." I feel sure he would rather be called "the Friend of sinners" than any of the fancy names sentimentalists have dreamed up for him.

It is a fact too seldom remembered that Jesus invariably saw the best in a person. If there was any good there at all, no matter how deeply buried it might be, if there was even a spark of goodness, he saw it. He saw it in Mary Magdalene. He saw it in Zacchaeus and Matthew, in the woman of

Samaria—five times married though she was—even in the thief on the cross!

How different he is in this from us. Too often we are ready to believe the worst of a person. There are some who are not only ready to believe the worst but spend their time looking for it. It has been said that "some people will believe anything —just so long as it is whispered to them."

Jesus always saw the best in a person; what do you see? Let us say, for instance, that you are seated in a hotel lobby and a complete stranger comes in and sits down opposite you. What do you see? How do you look at him? Do you look at him critically, noticing that his shoes are unshined, the hair carelessly combed, the suit somewhat in need of a pressing, the socks wrinkled; or do you tend to look at him with friendly interest and to think that, despite some unfavorable external evidence, he seems to be a decent sort, perhaps a potential friend?

What we see in a person is often not so much a revelation of the person as of ourselves. Thomas Carlyle looked at his own nation and said, "England has a population of 40 million people, mainly fools." That tells you something about Carlyle, doesn't it? David Livingstone, the great explorer-missionary, looked at Africa and said, "An unhappy people to whom I must dedicate my life." See the difference in the two men revealed in their outlook. What we see in others is often a greater revelation of ourselves than it is of the person looked at.

It is interesting to discover that Jesus saw the best in a

person. We usually think of him as the inflexible opponent of wrong. We know that he looked deep into the lives of men and clearly saw every weakness and every failure. We think that, because he knows us better than we know ourselves; knows the sordid, ugly and shameful things, he will therefore condemn us. But, and this is the wonder of his love, though every man's inner life stands starkly revealed to Jesus' penetrating insight, he loves us and, even more incredible, he believes in us!

Let this be clearly understood: God does not love only those who seem deserving, He loves *all* men—good and bad, saint and sinner. Recall to mind that familiar verse from Sunday School days, "God so loved the world"—not part of it, not the people in it, but *the world*—"that he gave his only begotten Son. . . ." Then let us learn this: God loves us, *all* of us, no matter who we are or how grievously we may have sinned, He loves us and He has faith in us!

The reason God believes in us where others may not is because He sees us differently. For instance, I look and see you as you are; God sees "the possible you." I see what is, God sees what can be. I see the outward appearance, God sees the heart. There was a much publicized series of cigarette advertisements not long ago that reiterated, "Believe in Yourself!" Well, most people do. No matter how frequently we may fail, deep within us we feel we can be better than we are. Well, so does God! Luther Burbank, America's great horticulturist, used to say, "Every weed is a potential flower." God says, "Every person is a potential saint."

It seems to me we have heard more than enough sermons on man's depravity. In other days the preacher labored to do one thing: to convince the hearer that he was a sinner. I want you to see the other side of the picture, I want you to see that God believes in you. He knows you better than you know yourself and He believes in you.

This is not to shut our eyes to the fact that there are failures in our lives that need forgiveness. We have all come short. We are reminded by Isaiah that "all we, like sheep, have gone astray. . . ." We have messed up our lives and lived other than our best. Jesus knew that, of course, and his constant emphasis was, "Go, and sin no more." But, and this is the point, when men and women came to Jesus conscious that they had failed he never added condemnation to condemnation. To the woman taken in adultery he said, "Neither do I condemn thee. Go, and sin no more." He did not denounce Mary Magdalene; he forgave her. He did not pour salt into the wounds of the thief on the cross; he said, "Today thou shalt be with me in Paradise." It is a fact that nowhere in the Bible record did Jesus denounce or recriminate any who came to him conscious of their failure and recognizing their need.

> The worst way to improve the world
> Is to condemn it.

It was not that he did not realize the enormity of their failure —it was just that he knew they knew they were wrong and he wanted them to know that he believed in them. And, just as you smile a smile out of a baby, his faith brought forth their faith and they were transformed.

Dr. Fosdick tells a story about a young man who came to him and poured out a brokenhearted tale of moral failure and defeat. When he was through, Dr. Fosdick said to him, "My friend, you are a fine-spirited, high-minded youth." Then the famous preacher continues, "I think I was never looked at with more startled eyes. 'Yes, you are a clean, fine-spirited, high-minded youth. That integrity is in you. If that were not in you, you would not be feeling the way you do about what you have done. You are a fine boy.'" Then he concludes, "I can hear him yet as he bowed himself down and wept . . ."

Michelangelo, the great sculptor, once bought an ugly piece of marble that no one else would buy. When asked why he had bought it—such an inferior piece—he squinted his artist's eyes and said, "Because there's an angel in there and I've got to set it free." Then he went to work with hammer and chisel and carved a magnificent statue of an angel. God looks deep into your life and says, "There's an angel there," and He wants to set it free.

Visiting in a home some years ago I saw a lusterless and ugly piece of quartz on a knickknack table in a corner. I asked the man of the house why he kept such an ordinary piece of rock in such a prominent place. He said, "Oh, it isn't ordinary. Come with me." We went out of doors and he held the rock between my eye and the direct rays of the sun. Suddenly it was a thing of beauty: sparkling, flashing, gleaming as though it were on fire. How ordinary it had seemed when first I saw it, just a chunk of ugly rock, and then the sun brought out all of its hidden beauty.

Huxley, the English scientist, tells us that everywhere in England, deep within the soil, are thousands of seeds of tropical plants. They have lain there dormant for years awaiting one thing, the moist warmth of a tropical climate. And if the climate of England could be changed they would immediately spring up into lush, beautiful foliage.

It is reported that when King Tut's tomb was opened a few years ago some wheat was discovered that had been there in the dry and dusty darkness for more than four thousand years. When it was brought out and planted, it grew and yielded a crop. All it needed was to get into the right relationship with the earth and the sun.

This is the need of our lives; to get them into a right relationship with the "Sun of Righteousness," to let the warmth of His love bring to birth within us new life and new usefulness. Then let the silent power of His love make you what you were made to be. There is a beauty within you, a strength of character, a power for good that no one has ever glimpsed—not even you. Jesus had a way of doing this with those who came to him. What a straggling little group his followers were. If there was any distinguishing thing about that early apostolic band it was their utter mediocrity. They were a perfect band of nobodies. Then Jesus found them and made them world changers. He saw in them a greatness that no other eyes could see, that they themselves had never seen, and he called it forth.

Across every century men have responded to the love of God that we see personified in Jesus Christ. How perfectly all of our lives, indeed, all of life, is pictured in a story Jesus told to illustrate God's love and man's response. We call it the story of the Prodigal Son. Literary critics have called it the greatest short story ever written. It has lived for centuries because it encompasses the entire story of man's relationship to God. Here we see the Father-child relationship of which Jesus spoke, the rebellion of the child against the Father's will, the poverty and emptiness of a life that selfishly seeks its own and the abundant forgiveness and reconciliation granted by the Father when, repentant, the child returns. This is the story of life.

The story lives because even the unthinking sense their identification with the prodigal. We know, as men have always known, that we are creatures and that we perish apart from the Creator. Yet we frequently act as though God were the enemy of our souls, as though we, children that we are, know better than the Father what is good for us. So we go our own way and the result may be seen in the internal discord and spiritual poverty of our lives. In the words of C. S. Lewis, "We are halfhearted creatures, fooling about with drink and sex and ambition when infinite joy is offered us, like an ignorant child who wants to go on making mud-pies in a slum because he cannot imagine what is meant by the offer of a holiday at sea. We are far too easily pleased."

God would effect a transformation in our lives if we would but let Him. As William James has said, "Every sort of energy and endurance, of courage and capacity for handling life's evils, is set free in those who have religious faith." But we are kept from the Father by our self-will. When the prodigal demands his inheritance and leaves his father his great concern is for himself. "Give *me* the portion of goods that are *mine*," he says. Later, when he returns, how different his words are. "I have sinned," he cries, "I am no longer worthy . . ."! What a change in emphasis! And we are as wrong as he was when the emphasis of our lives is "Give me . . . mine."

Selfishness is the fundamental sin and most of the problems of life grow out of this "give me" emphasis. The conflicts between individuals, the continuing clash between capital and labor, the ruthless expansionist movement of the imperialism of the past and the modern imperialism, communism, are examples of people and groups and nations crying, "Give me . . . mine!"

It is this consuming selfishness that lies back of strife and division and war. A man must provide for himself and his family, of course, but never at the expense of others. Jesus constantly made it clear that self-love is wrong unless one holds an equal love for one's neighbor. It is this consuming selfishness that bars us from God's love. He believes in us, but He knows He cannot bring us to fulfillment until we cease to believe in ourselves and put our faith in Him. It takes *two* believing to make a Christian; God believing in us and we in Him. So long as we assume the lordship of our own lives He can do nothing for us. He cannot give us

His love any more than a father can give his child an education. The father can provide the money and the opportunity
but he cannot *give* his child an education. The child must
will to receive it. So God cannot grant His forgiveness and
His grace unless we will to receive Him as the Lord of our
life.

There is an oft-told tale of a beggar who sat daily in the
street across from an artist's studio. From the window the
artist painted a portrait of the beggar and then one day called
him in to see it. At first the beggar did not recognize himself.
"Who is it?" he kept asking, while the artist stood watching
him and smiling. Then, as recognition began to dawn, he
asked half-doubting, "Is it me? Can it be me?" "That's the
man as I see him," replied the artist. Then the beggar made
a magnificent response. "If that's the man you see," he said,
"that's the man I'll be!"

God sees something in all of us, something invisible to
every eye but His. Only God could see the possibilities in
such a man as Matthew, for instance. We call him St.
Matthew but he was anything but a saint when Jesus called
him from his roadside booth to immortality. Matthew was
a publican, a tax collector. In twentieth-century phraseology,
he was a "quisling," a "collaborationist." He was a Jew who
worked for the hated Roman government extorting taxes from
his own people. The publicans of that day were invariably
corrupt (a relatively honest publican died and they carved
on his headstone, "Here Lies an Honest Publican." He was
such an exception it was not necessary to include his name.)

So rapacious were these men that the rabbis would grant pious Jews the right to swear out their income-tax returns improperly, to protect them from the avarice of these greedy and unprincipled men. The Jews despised the publicans. They would spit on the ground as they passed their places of business. Publicans were not allowed to live in the Jewish community, but dwelt outside of the town with the lepers. They were social outcasts, the lowest of the low. Such a man was Matthew; a greedy, money-grubbing, avaricious, collaborating quisling! Then he met Jesus. The Master passed by his taxbooth and called out, "Follow me." Matthew arose, turned his back on the old way of life and began to follow him. And now we call him St. Matthew, and every century has been blessed by the book that bears his name.

God sees something in us invisible to all eyes but His. He sees possibilities in the most hopeless. He sees a potential purity in the most confirmed blackguard. He sees the saint within every sinner. He believes in us. Dare we put our faith in Him that His faith in us may be realized?

God stands waiting to move into any life that will surrender itself to Him. He never commits Himself to triflers; to those who would have their God as a servant and their religion as a convenience. But when we admit the emptiness of life without Him, when we confess our need and the failure of our best resolves, then—even as Christ has promised—He comes flooding into our drab lives bringing power and beauty and meaning.

❧ 13 ❧

MAKING RELIGION REAL

Most of us have longed at some time or another for some striking evidence that there is a God. How often have we thought, "If only God would reveal Himself in unquestionable reality. If only there could be for us as there was for men in ancient times a sign or a vision." Many of us are like a woman who went to her minister and said, "I have been in the church for years. I believe in God and try to serve Him, yet, to be perfectly candid, God isn't real to me. What can I do?"

There can be no doubt but what the faith of many moderns has a nebulous quality. It would never occur to them to question the central beliefs of the church; they accept the creeds without serious question, they have a little flower of worship within them and they water it at least once a week, but their religion is an unreal thing. Prayer is time put in as a necessary duty or the last resort in time of trouble. Church attendance is a habit. The Bible is a respected but little understood book and God is dim, distant and unreal.

But there have been others whose faith was a very different thing. So certain of their faith were Jesus' disciples that, tradition relates, all of them save one gladly died as martyrs. In

171

subsequent generations thousands died in Roman arenas. Rent by wild animals or wrapped in a blanket of flame they sang in their agony. Who can doubt that God was real to Augustine when he turned from his life of sensuality to give his amazing intellect to the church, to Francis of Assisi when he turned from his frivolous prodigality to dedicate himself with unparalleled devotion, to Livingstone of Africa, to Grenfell of Labrador, to Wesley of England, to a countless host of others who have lived and died for their faith? History makes it plain that to these their faith was more important than life itself and in the confident assurance that God was with them they dedicated themselves to Him even at the cost of their own pleasure and privilege.

How may we know such certainty? Is it possible in our kind of world? May we, after centuries of scientific achievement, when many a cherished belief has become untenable, find a similar certainty?

We begin our quest for certainty by ridding our mind of the idea that God will be apprehended through any or all of the five senses. There will be no vision seen, no voice heard, no tangible substance touched. The seeker for God must realize that there will be no sign in the sky, no voice in the wind, no spectral materialization. The testimony of all who have apprehended God authenticates the statement of Jesus, "God is a Spirit (not substance): and they that worship him must worship him in spirit and in truth."

This rather negative beginning may make Christian experience seem vague and unreal. Our difficulty lies in the fact that in an age dominated by materialism we are confused as to the nature of reality. We commonly assume that the things we can see and feel and weigh and measure are the real things. We say, "Solid as the rock of Gibraltar, permanent as the mountains, ageless as the pyramids." It is a fact, however, that all of these apparently permanent things will someday crumble and disintegrate. The only things that actually last, that truly are ageless, are the intangibles. It was this fact to which the Apostle Paul had reference when he said, "The things which are seen are temporal; but the things which are not seen are eternal."

What was it, for instance, that seemed to be the dominant fact in the world some two thousand years ago? It was Rome was it not? Rome with her military might, her magnificent buildings, her spreading Empire. The truth, the ideals and the love of which Jesus spoke seemed trivial by comparison. Whose influence really counts, Caesar's or Jesus'? Look at Caesar. Marshal his legions around him, pile up his wealth and power, call out his conquests. Then look at Jesus. Gather around him his little ragged band of nobodies, study his poverty, watch the soldiers as they beat the life out of him, see him as his bloody body sags upon the cross. Pit Jesus against the Dictator?—it is like trying to stop a tank with the splintering wood of a cross!

And yet, where is Caesar's might today? His armies are history, his buildings lie in ruins, his influence is nil. The only things of that time that still abide are the ideas that were held. The things of which Jesus spoke and which his life exemplified, these apparently unreal things, have outlasted the material world in which they were first stated and grow stronger with each century.

There is evidence all about us to testify to the reality of the things commonly regarded as unreal. For instance, who among us has ever *seen* an idea? Are ideas therefore unimportant? On the contrary, we have seen the transformation an idea can work in the life of a man when it takes possession of him. Think of what an idea did in the life of Columbus, the Wright brothers, Martin Luther, the Founding Fathers, Thomas Edison, Albert Einstein! Are ideas real?—our very world is shaped by them. The war between Communism and the West is fundamentally a clash of ideas.

Who has ever *seen* love? No one of course, but what a power it is! How it changes those it touches. How it engenders unselfishness and sacrifice. It makes possible our homes and our society. There could be no life as we know it without this intangible we call love.

Who has ever *seen* faith? Ridiculous question. But we have seen what faith can do. It undergirds, directs and empowers our lives. It produces patience and fortitude. Anyone who has studied history knows well that faith is essential to life.

The real things in the world are the invisible spiritual realities. Is it so difficult, then, to believe in God? We may not apprehend Him with our finite perceptions but this does not mean He does not exist. It simply means that He exists in a realm beyond our ken. If we would worship Him we must, in Jesus' words, "worship him in spirit and in truth."

In our quest for certainty we must rid our mind of another misconception: that God is known through the acceptance of a creed. Across the centuries the Christian Church has believed certain things about God and, for convenience, has formulated a number of creeds. No creed is sacrosanct, but if ideas and beliefs are to be passed on to succeeding generations they must needs be stated. Unfortunately, many have believed that the aim of the Church is to get men and women to render assent to a creed. But the mere acquiescence to a set of propositions about God does not bring a person to God. Christianity would be a dull and stultifying thing indeed if it were simply a matter of accepting a new set of ideas, a new frame of reference, a new philosophy of life.

We must see clearly that Christianity is not, primarily, a philosophy or a set of rules for living. Essentially it is a relationship, a friendship, an experience, a way of life. This does not mean that it is irrational, or that it does not have the elements of a philosophy. It does not mean that Christian experience is an entirely subjective business. It does mean that it is a personal relationship of trust in God, a heart-warming consciousness that in response to your faith in God there has been a divine-human encounter in which you have come to know Him, "whom to know is life eternal."

We must disabuse ourselves of yet another idea: that certainty may be found by what is termed the scientific method, by the judicious weighing of all the evidence. One will never discover God who looks for Him only in the realm of logic and concrete evidence. God cannot be "proved." There are a great many convincing arguments by which one may attempt to demonstrate the fact of God but they are not conclusive. You can no more "prove" God than you can "prove" beauty. It may be argued that a certain painting or piece of music is beautiful but if it does not so seem to you no argument will convince you. In the last analysis beauty is something known by experience. By the same token God is known, ultimately, by experience.

There are many who clamor for a definition of God. You can no more define God than you can catch a fragrant spring breeze in a paper bag. Catch the breeze in the bag and what do you have when you examine it—a fragrant spring breeze? No, you have a sackful of stale air! Catch God in a definition and what do you have—God? No, you have some inadequate human terms, invented by men to describe their common experiences, and, by their nature, utterly incapable of describing the infinite. We will not find the reality we seek by the use of the scientific method.

How then may we find spiritual certainty? It is at this point that the merely curious will be disappointed. It may be that you have been following along in the expectation of some simple answer. But there are no pat little formulas to tell a man how he may certainly find God.

Assuredly there are conditions to be met, and the first is a deep and absorbing concern. We do not find God as we might find a coin while walking down the road. There must be the recognition of our inadequacy. We must sense our need. We must seek if we would find. The words of Moses remain true across the years, "If . . . thou shalt seek the Lord thy God, thou shalt find him, *if* thou seek him with all thy heart and with all thy soul."

Let us recognize, first, that God may be found in nature.

> The heavens declare the glory of God;
> And the firmament sheweth his handiwork.

There are few places where God speaks so meaningfully as in the breathtaking beauty of the world round about us. Which of us has never been overwhelmed with wonder at the fragrant greenness of the spring, the indescribable color of the fall, the restless mysterious majesty of the waves breaking over the rocks, the incredibly delicate shading of a flower, the deep clear wells of a child's eyes? Who is so insensitive that he has never heard the voice of nature whisper . . . "God!"

> In the rustling grass
> I hear Him pass.

But it is not enough to glimpse God in the myriad beauties of nature. The God of beauty may be found there and the God of law and order, but not the God of love. Nature is beautiful and orderly but nature is also cruel, "red in tooth and claw." The God seen in nature is impersonal and indifferent. The waters are beautiful but they will drown you, the beneficent sun will burn you, the graceful beast will claw you, the gentle snow will freeze you. You do not find the God of love in nature.

You may also catch a glimpse of God in the experiences of everyday life. To those who have eyes to see, God is in every vista. To those who are tuned to hear, His "still small voice" whispers in every sound. God is found not only in church or at the communion table or at some "holy place." In Bible times men and women were constantly finding Him in diverse and unexpected places. The Wise Men found Him in a stable, Simeon found Him in the Temple, the disciples found Him in the solitary place, the thief found Him on a cross! You never knew for sure just where you would come upon Him. It is so today. God knocks at the door of our lives in a thousand ways and never twice the same.

We may find God in special moments of crisis. It is when a man gets to the end of his rope that God gets through to him. It is a sad commentary on human nature but it is true. Most of us give little thought to God in times of prosperity and peace but when life drives us to our knees we begin to pray. How inconsistent we are; let things go well and we take the credit—"Oh what a bright boy am I"—but let life go awry and we begin to cry, "How could God let this happen to me?"

We tend to think that God is found only through meditation or worship or prayer. That He reveals Himself to those who seek Him thus is undoubtedly true, but He is often found far from the sanctuary. We meet Him not only in the secret place but also in the market place.

How might a man have found the Christ child on that gray December night centuries ago? We have long been critical of the Innkeeper who turned the travel-stained couple from the door. "No room in the Inn."—how familiar the words are. And yet, have you not said to yourself, How could the Innkeeper know? How could this harassed man be expected to know this woman bore the Divine Babe within her swollen body? How could he know?

Well there *were* some who knew! The shepherds did not miss Him—but then they were out in the solitude and had learned the secrets of the silence. Simeon and Anna did not miss Him—but then they were always in the temple athrill with the anticipation of God's entrance into history. The Wise Men did not miss Him—but then they had an eye to the wisdom of God as well as the wisdom of men.

How could you have found Him back there? Someone concerned about the needs of others might have found Him on coming to the stable to lend a hand to the poor. Someone worried about wanderers with no place to go on a bleak December night might have found Him for whom there was no room in the Inn. Someone with a love for children might have found Him, drawn by the cry of a baby in the night. Years later, someone interested in helping criminals might have found Him between two thieves on a cross!

Do we not miss Him simply because we are unmoved by the needs of others? According to Jesus He looks out from the eyes of the poor, the sick, the unhoused, the hungry. If you would find Him seek out the underprivileged, the sick, the dispossessed. "Inasmuch as ye have done it unto one of the least of these . . . ye have done it unto me," Jesus said. Have a care then lest in seeking Him in prayer or pilgrimage you pass Him by. He is just around the corner, He is in the slum section of your city, He is in that hospital you pass every day. If you will seek Him there you will find Him . . . in jail!

Then begin to seek Him. Make this "Project Number One" in your life. Our days are so jampacked with a thousand tasks and involvements that we have almost crowded out the worthwhile things. Real living takes time. You cannot hope to find faith in a frantic five minutes sandwiched between appointments. It takes time. God is not a pleasant little "extra" in life, He is central, and if you would know Him you must seek Him with all your heart.

God stands waiting to move into any life that will surrender itself to Him. He never commits Himself to triflers; to those who would have their God as a servant and their religion as a convenience. But when we admit the emptiness of life without Him, when we confess our need and the failure of our best resolves, then—even as Christ has promised—He comes flooding into our drab lives bringing power and beauty and meaning.

*What a difference the resurrection makes!
Look at the scene on Friday and all you
can see is failure. But look again on
Sunday and all is changed. Christ has
taken the Cross and, using it as a battering-ram, has driven the end out of the
sepulcher to let in the light of an eternal
day.*

❦ 14 ❦

THE END IS THE BEGINNING

THE city of Jerusalem is silent. Citizen and stranger are deep in sleep. In the palace, between silken sheets, the governor tosses fitfully. At his post, propped against the wall, a Roman legionnaire dozes, his spear slipping from his relaxing fingers. In their simple or elaborate houses the Jews sleep. In their tents and beneath the open sky the pilgrims sleep, gathering strength for the long journey homeward. Rich and poor, camel driver and high priest, in elegant bedchamber or on a rough sack of reeds, the city sleeps. There is no movement but the gentle rustle of the palm branches and the labored breathing of an animal. The Passover is finished. The throbbing excitement of the past few days is over and the chill, silent stars spangle the dark blanket of blue that covers a city asleep.

But no. In the pale, yellow light of the oncoming dawn a solitary figure emerges from the gate of the city. It is a woman, bent and frail. Her hands are clutched as in unutterable grief and there are tears on her face as, with her shadow skulking jerkily behind her, she slips silently down the sandy slope, crosses the River Kedron and plods up the hill on the other side.

It is Mary Magdalene.

What an utter tragedy Christ's death must have been to Mary. He had done so much for her. She had been so low and he had brought her so high. Before she had met him she had known little but baseness and squalor, and then he had taken her by the hand and lifted her and since that time she had even been able to respect herself.

Now all of this was gone. Jesus was dead! There before her eyes he had died. As she watched him he had died. No words of love in his ears but only the hoarse sounds of hate hammering at his head. How she wished she could have slipped past the restraining pikes of the Roman soldiery and, running forward until her sandals sank in the fresh-dug earth at the foot of the cross, looked up into his face to cry out her devotion. If only she could have let him know that though the others had fled she had not. But now it was too late and there was nothing she could do but to come before the city stirred to the place where he was buried to hold a lonely vigil by the door of the tomb.

Many a woman has known the grief that Mary knew: the leaden-hearted despairing numbness of bereavement. She holds that in common with all who have lost a loved one. But Mary knew something else. She knew, not only the pang of death, but the unutterable, devastating joy of resurrection! There by the tomb she came upon the resurrected Christ, finding him as we often do in life, unexpectedly and in the midst of despair. Suddenly, in the half-darkness there was a figure standing in the deeper shadows, then a familiar voice, then the one word . . . "Mary." She thought she would faint in the sudden, glad bewilderment that flooded through her body and sped her feet to his side! "Rabboni!" she cried. "Oh my Master . . . !"

I doubt if any of us, separated as we are by the centuries from the scene of the resurrection, can begin to comprehend the utter tragedy that prefaced that unforgettable dawn. For the struggling little group who had been following Jesus the world had come to an end. All their high hopes had been suddenly and irrevocably dashed. Their whole world had come tumbling down about them and lay in ruins at their feet. Jesus was dead! Jesus, their leader, their incomparable master, their trusted friend, their guide, their *God* . . . was dead!

And what hopes they had built up around him. He had found them living out their drab little lives and had transformed them. They followed and watched him as miracles seemed to flow from his fingers and unheard-of wisdom fell from his lips. They saw the swelling throngs that crowded him. They heard the "Hosannas" that his coming raised. They stood in awe as he confronted and confounded the Pharisees.

Then they began to dream dreams about a Kingdom. He would put away Rome as he had put away disease. He would bring good times even as he had provided bread for the thousands in the wilderness. There would be wealth for all and power for all and freedom for all, and Israel would assume her rightful place in the sun. There would be a throne for Jesus of course, and possibly other thrones too, and were they not his most trusted lieutenants, his closest friends . . . ?

Then, all of a sudden, the whole world collapsed. Jesus was dead! Dead of all places on a cross—a shameful, criminal's cross. They saw the blood on Him, the crown of thorns, the death in His eyes and the shattering agony in his face. They saw the gleam of light on the pikes and spears of the soldiers and their flesh crawled with the thought that they might be next. It was then they ran. Ran through the echoing, sinister streets to places of hiding, to bolt the doors behind them and to lie palpitating in the darkness with the rude cries from Calvary sifting through to them from the distance.

What tragedy! What utter failure! Today we call it "Good Friday"; to the disciples it was the blackest of history's evil days. What a bitter cup! They had expected to see Jesus ascend to a throne; instead, they had seen him nailed to a cross.

And then . . . the resurrection! What a difference the resurrection makes! Look at the scene on Friday and all you can see is failure. But look again on Sunday and all is changed. Christ has taken the Cross and, using it as a battering-ram, has driven the end out of the sepulcher to let in the light of an eternal day. The grave has become a gateway. Death is now a door. The tombstone has become a milestone and the graveyard has become a brighter place, festooned about with hope. Christ, the Divine Samson, has picked up the iron gates of impossibility and has carried them off. What a difference the resurrection makes. What a difference in the life of Mary and the disciples. What a difference in the history of the world.

Across the centuries hundreds of arguments have been marshaled in an attempt to prove the fact of the resurrection.

It is impossible, of course, to prove it beyond contradiction. The event transpired centuries ago and any indisputable evidence is gone beyond recall. Moreover it is not my purpose here to argue. Some may be won to faith by arguments but they are few. There are many arguments that may be adduced —arguments from the scriptures, from nature, by analogy— but religious debate is a sterile sort of business usually carried on with more heat than light and it is not our concern here.

But while we are not concerned to "prove" the fact of the resurrection or to argue about the manner in which Christ came from the grave, it would seem that it is necessary to see the importance of the resurrection because of the implications that flow from it. There are some who contend it does not matter whether it is a fact or not, but it would appear to be absolutely central to Christian faith. The Apostle Paul states it succinctly: "If Christ be not risen, then is our preaching vain, and your faith is also vain."

The resurrection is important because the Christian religion is based on the faith that Christ was right about the nature of the universe. If he was wrong we are fools to follow him. To quote Paul again: "If Christ be not risen then is our preaching vain, and your faith is also vain . . . and we are of all men most miserable!" Jesus predicted his resurrection and if he was wrong about this he may well have been wrong about everything else.

Jesus said in a hundred ways that, at its heart, the universe is friendly. He taught that God can best be described by the word "Father." In parables and direct statement he said there is meaning to life, that things do not "just happen" as the result of sheer chance and that behind the scenes God stands in control of history. He was either right or wrong. If Christ was not vindicated after his death it means this: it means he was wrong about life and that God either does not care or does not exist. It means that if there is a God at all He is impersonal, detached and utterly indifferent to justice or suffering or goodness. It means that all morality is a fool's dream. It means that Pilate was right in getting this troublemaker out of the way. It means that the Founding Fathers were naïve when they wrote on their coins, "In God We Trust," and that this business about all men being endowed with equal rights is just so much nonsense. If Jesus was wrong then Hitler was right; he just was not strong enough. It means that all of life is indeed "a tale told by an idiot, full of sound and fury, signifying nothing."

Think it through. That is what it means. For if Jesus was wrong then there is no God—at least no personal God—and, that being so, then the Communists are at least realistic and on what grounds do we criticize them? It is precisely because God is the ground of all morality that churchmen, statesmen and scientists are calling for a moral and spiritual revival in America. The resurrected Christ is the evidence that God is at the heart of life, that evil will not triumph and that life has meaning. It is central to our faith.

What a difference the resurrection makes! What a difference in our view of the future. Who can doubt now that God holds the future in His hand? Hydrogen bomb or no, communism, hate, war or no. Let men rail and contrive, the future is God's. How we need this certainty today. The world is shot through with fear and apprehension. What fear of the future: of tomorrow's wars, of the possibility of total destruction. Our world is like a ship which has slipped its mooring in the night and in the morning there is no land in sight, the sun and stars are obscured, the compass is broken, the rudder smashed and the captain dead.

There is no serenity if we face the future without Christ. There are no ultimate answers apart from him. We seem to have found all the answers except the important ones. We are wise enough to create the Bomb but not good enough to be trusted with it. We had thought that science would be our savior and that knowledge would bring wisdom but now we are beginning to realize that the banishment of ignorance is not enough. Knowledge is not goodness. A clever mind may be an evil mind. As Fulton Sheen has suggested, "All you do when you educate some men is to turn a stupid devil into a clever devil"—and thus make him more dangerous. Is this not precisely our predicament: we have failed to match our scientific and technological progress with our moral progress until now we have created a Frankenstein monster that bids fair to destroy its creator?

There seems to be a fundamental perversity in the heart of mankind. Give us printing presses with which to put good books within the reach of every man and we will build larger presses to flood the newsstands with pornography, comics and Mickey Spillane. Give us television sets to provide information and recreation and we will crowd it with low comedy and bloody up the screen with crime. Shrink our world with improved transportation and communication and we make our very proximity our danger. There is a fatal flaw in all of our planning: we have been leaving God out, and the future promises nothing but confusion compounded without Him. The resurrection is the demonstration that "in everything God works for good with those who love Him," and that the future is in His hands.

What a difference the resurrection made in the lives of the disciples! Before that first Easter they had been quarrelsome, vacillating, self-seeking men, afterward they are like men aflame. How do we account for the transformation in their lives? There *is* no explaining it apart from some tremendous event in their midst—the validation of all they had haltingly believed when Jesus was among them. They had been doubting and craven before but now nothing can intimidate them, not even threats of prison, pain and death. What if they did have crosses to bear?—if God could do this with Christ's cross what could He not do with theirs! In the midst of their despair they had seen the resurrected Christ and they knew beyond question that the final answers lie with God. No tragedy can quench their hopes; they have seen Calvary culminate in the empty tomb. Even death is not the end; they have seen the resurrected Christ. What can you do to intimidate them? Do your worst and they know that if God be for them who can be against them. Everything is in a different perspective now, and they go out to turn the world upside down.

What a difference the resurrection makes in our confidence in Christ. He comes back from "the valley of the shadow" to say, "There is nothing to fear." He had said, "Lo, I am with you always," and the promise had been kept. Who can doubt his promises now?

It is little wonder that across the centuries Jesus' words have strengthened men and women, for his is the voice of experience. He has perfectly identified himself with each of us in every experience of life. There is no grief, no trouble, no problem that he has not faced and conquered. Do you know tears?—he wept them too: hot, blinding tears at the grave of his friend Lazarus, heartbroken tears over the wayward Jerusalem. Are you friendless?—who has ever been more alone than he who "came unto his own and they received him not," who hung forsaken on a cross and in his agony cried out even to God, "Why hast *thou* forsaken me?" Are you tempted?—who has ever known temptation as he faced it in the wilderness? Are you bereaved?—think of what he did for Jairus and the Widow of Nain. Are you sick?—he is the Great Physician.

May it not be that the reason Christ came into the world as a babe and grew to full maturity was so that he might perfectly understand the needs of all men? When a child stammers its first lisping prayer, Christ understands for he was once a child. When a teenager comes to him, facing the tensions and conflicts of adolescence, he understands for he was once a teenager. When we come to him in the full maturity of adulthood, he understands for he lived in this world as a man.

Why should we doubt him then? In the resurrected Christ we see one who has come back from the ultimate grapple of life and his first word is "Peace." Why should we despair then? Why should we draw back and be afraid? Why should there be a tempest in our souls? The victorious, risen Christ returns to say, "Peace."

Finally, notice what a difference the resurrection may make in our own lives. The final test of the Christian Gospel is not "What does it say?" or "What does it claim?" or "How reasonable is it?"—but what can it accomplish in our lives? Away with the churches, Bibles, creeds, hymns, choirs and all the paraphernalia of religion if they do not echo a message that makes life different, unless—in a way no theologian can explain—they reflect the God who enters into human life to transform it. There is no purpose to Christianity, no meaning to all this going on about God and salvation unless in the divine-human encounter we are changed.

This is the miracle of Easter, the miracle of human transformation! Mary Magdalene is the miracle of Easter; she and everyone else like her who has found a transformed life through the resurrected Christ. I know something of what power it takes to transform human life. I have lived long enough and have dealt with men and women long enough to know what a grip the habits of the years can get on a person, and how weak mere human resolve is in the face of it. And when I see what Mary Magdalene has become, and remember what she used to be I stand in hushed awe in the presence of God.

And what he did for Mary he can do for us. The resurrection happened two thousand years ago, but has it happened to *you?*